GRAHAM JONES

Own Goals

A Devastating Collection of Self-inflicted Disasters, Blunders and Super-goofs

CENTURY PUBLISHING
LONDON

ACKNOWLEDGEMENTS

The author would like to thank all the friends who have crossed his palm with stories, the publishers of Britain's nine daily and eight Sunday newspapers, two American and six British weekly magazines, and the plethora of book publishers too numerous to mention here for the raw material which is the basis for this volume. Anyone who feels the author has committed an 'own goal' by not giving further acknowledgement is invited to contact the publishers. It is anticipated that any significant omission of credit for material used will be corrected in future editions.

Cover illustration, pop-up illustration and cartoons by David Mostyn
Pop-up mechanics by Jonathan Biggs

First published in Great Britain in 1985
by Century Publishing Co. Ltd,
Portland House,
12–13 Greek Street, London W1V 5LE

British Library Cataloguing in Publication Data

Jones, Graham, *1951*–
Own goals: a devastating collection of self-
inflicted disasters, blunders and super-goofs.
I. Title
828'.91409   PR6060.O516/

ISBN 0 7126 0714 5

Photoset by Rowland Phototypesetting Ltd
Bury St Edmunds, Suffolk
Printed in Great Britain in 1985 by
Purnell & Sons (Book Production) Ltd, Paulton, Bristol

Contents

Boomerangs for the Boys in Blue – Forces Favourites – Military Own Goals – 10 Five-Star Own Goals in Battle – Officialdom – 20 Pitfalls for Politicos and Those in Public Life

.

DEDICATION

This book is dedicated to goalkeepers and journalists everywhere (the risks are about the same). And to the players, staff and supporters of Halifax Town football club. If anyone needs cheering up, you do.

Introduction

The Scotland Yard chiefs who met for a reunion dinner at London's Connaught Rooms . . . only to find, when they left, thirteen of their cars had been towed away.

Jim Chanda Wape of Zimbabwe, who bricked himself into the annexe he was building. He only got out when a driver called with still more bricks and had to knock the wall down for his signature.

The torpedo which misfired . . . and biffed into a Royal Navy frigate in the Firth of Clyde.

The couple who emigrated from Britain because they wanted to get away from the ever-present threat of war. They chose . . . the Falkland Islands. ✓

This is the world of own goals. Boomerangs. Super-bloopers. Ultra gaffes. Actions which rebounded mightily, savagely – but always amusingly – on their makers.

Political own goals, sporting own goals, showbiz own goals, here is every category of self-inflicted misery. Stupendous clangers, horrendous *doubles entendres*, cruel accidents to the famous and not-so-famous.

Albatross phrases that bounced back to haunt world leaders. Travellers who found themselves on the wrong side of the world by mistake. Robbers who blundered their way straight into jail, critics who belittled future super-stars, predictions which went totally wrong. The items have two things in common: Yes, they're funny. But Ouch! they hurt.

There was parking superintendent George Lawrence, who failed to recognise Princess Anne at the Horse of the Year Show. He told her to get out of her car 'and walk just like everyone else'.

√ Undertaker Michael Batchelor of Twickenham who put £1250 in a coffin 'for safekeeping'. It was cremated by mistake.

And perhaps the most typical own goal of all: the travel agents who arranged a conference in Spain to discuss the problem of over-booking. When they arrived at their hotel they found themselves . . . double booked.

DON'T EVER LET IT HAPPEN TO YOU!

Ouch! or, Trapped by a Rather Delicate Part of One's Anatomy

Accidents do happen, and most could be avoided. Try telling that to club singer Ian Whittaker, who was prancing round the room with tears in his eyes as the ambulancemen arrived.

Wearing only his underpants, and looking for a screwdriver, poor Mr Whittaker, of Oswaldtwistle, Lancs, forgot to stand back when he slammed the drawer on his wife's sewing machine. He was caught by that part Scotsmen usually hide under their kilt.

His wife Maureen, 28, said: 'He opened the drawer and slammed it shut on himself. He was in absolute agony. But the ambulancemen, bless them, tried their best not to laugh when I told them how he did it.'

David Webb, 34, of Doncaster, came to grief in April 1982 after he spent the evening watching videos of his hero, Superman. He woke up in the back garden in his pyjamas, suffering agonies from a dislocated jaw, cracked ribs and bruises. Dreaming he himself was Superman, he had 'flown' out of the bedroom window in his sleep.

Public and social engagements are a minefield for the unwary. One slip can mean instant ridicule. The deadlier the faux-pas, the worse it is for the gaffer: the funnier it is for the rest of us. There was Mrs Thatcher, who, touring a firm of electrical repairers in West London, in April 1983, pointed to a huge screwdriver and said loudly: 'What a peculiar tool. I've never seen one quite as large as that.' Collapse of her audience.

There was Nancy Reagan, who, during the 1980 presidential

campaign, gushed: 'It's wonderful to see all these beautiful white faces . . . er . . . I mean black and white faces.'

Though one of the funniest slips came from another one-time presidential contender, Senator Barry Goldwater. When asked by American chat host Joey Bishop if he would like to become a regular on the show, he replied: 'No thank you. I'd much rather watch you in bed with my wife.'

That brings us neatly on to politics, and an own goal with heavier repercussions: President Richard Nixon on coast-to-coast TV in April 1974 to announce he was handing over the White House tapes. 'In giving you these records, blemishes and all,' he said, 'I am placing my trust in the fairness of the American people.'

There was John F. Kennedy's decision to offer the Vice-Presidential nomination to one Lyndon B. Johnson, apparently in the safe knowledge he would refuse. He didn't. Said JFK without much foresight: 'I don't see any reason in the world why he should want it.'

A little while later came Ronald Reagan, who had to have intensive schooling to try and prise his foot out of his mouth. 'How did I know the B-1 bomber was an airplane?' wailed the chief in July 1982. 'I thought it was vitamins for the troops.'

While on the subject of political self-humblement we should mention:

IAN SPROAT, minister in the Conservative government until 1983. After boundary changes he left his marginal constituency Aberdeen South for a safer seat at the June 1983 election. Unfortunately he lost his new stomping ground of Roxburgh and Berwickshire to a Liberal. The Tory who followed him in Aberdeen South romped home by 3500 votes.

EFRAIN RIOS MONTT, President of Guatemala, who in August 1983, dismissed rumours of a coup as 'so many hairs in the soup'. He was toppled two days later.

And PRESIDENT SEBE of the Ciskei. He bought a lavish executive jet for his own personal use – but was forced to keep it across the border in South Africa. His country did not have a runway long enough for it to land.

Some of the funniest own-goals come from the bungling of criminals. There was Thomas Crehan of Wolverhampton who broke into a bank in 1982, then had to dial 999 when he found he couldn't get out. He told police: 'I'm in Lloyds, by the safe.'

Also in 1982 there was the vain forger of Kenya who instead of putting the president's picture on counterfeit banknotes used a portrait of himself. While armed robber Kenneth Nelson, after being sentenced to fifteen years jail, sarcastically told the judge at Portland, Oregon: 'Go ahead and pile it on – see if I care.' The judge happily obliged and gave him two consecutive thirty-year terms – sixty years in jail in all. It took Nelson eleven years to get his sentence reduced.

Even more daffy was blabbermouth bank robber Bill Gillen of Glasgow. Police called him in for an identification parade in the spring of 1983, but he became upset when the bank teller who had pursued him walked right past. 'Don't you recognise me?' he shouted. 'I'm the man you chased.'

Officialdom often has cause to say 'Ouch!' There was the US National Academy of Design, who awarded second prize in an art competition to a work by Edward Dickinson. Then someone let on to the judges that all the time it had been hanging upside down.

There were blushes too at Essex County Council's public

relations office in May, 1976, after the council put out a press release on adult illiteracy. They hadn't been able to spell the word 'illiterate'.

Government servants should be careful what they send out. Defending a man accused of sending obscene material through the post, a lawyer in Norfolk, Virginia, asked the US Justice Department for a copy. It arrived two days later . . . through the post.

From civil servants to the police. There was the kindly bobby who stopped traffic at the ten-mile mark in a marathon in July 1972, and waved all the runners on. Unfortunately he sent the entire 127-strong field in the Windsor to Chiswick 26-mile road race in the wrong direction. It took race marshals, police cars and motorcyclists nearly an hour to round up all the runners.

It can happen to all ranks. Take Sir Colin Woods, newly-appointed head of Australia's federal police force. Two weeks after he arrived from Britain to begin a crackdown on crime in June 1979 . . . his wallet was stolen.

Spanish police rushed to the scene when they were alerted that a bank robbery was taking place in the north-west port of Vigo, in 1984. What followed was like something out of the Keystone Kops.

One policeman shot off his own toe, another jumped from the police car – which had broken down – and gave himself concussion. The third was knocked out cold – with his own gun.

From police to the military. Spare a thought for the Flight Lieutenant of the RAF aerobatic team The Red Arrows who in 1969 reacted quickly to the radio order: 'You are on fire, Eject!' He baled out safely and as he floated gracefully down to earth, watched his £400 000 Folland Gnat plane smash into the ground and disintegrate. There was just one problem. The radio order had been meant for another pilot.

In February 1971 2500 American radio and TV stations received a signal that the country was on nuclear war alert. Some stations went off the air after broadcasting the warning. Others just carried on and hoped for the best.

The message, put out by Associated Press and UPI, contained the code word 'hatefulness' which identified it as genuine. At the National Warning Centre, deep inside Cheyenne Mountain, Colorado, an official said that the warning had been inadvertently transmitted by a civilian operator who thought he was running a test tape. He said 'I can't imagine how the hell it happened'.

That was also US Defence Secretary Caspar Weinberger's response to hearing of the execution of General Bill E. Goat. In July 1983 General Goat was the mascot of the US marines in Lebanon and had been scrubbed, decorated and groomed before being given a VIP ride back from Beirut to be adopted by an 11-year-old girl. They shouldn't have bothered. Agriculture Department officials decreed the goatee general a possible carrier of disease. He had no reservation at the quarantine centre at Kennedy Airport, and ruling 'no exceptions', they ordered him to be put down forthwith.

Man's insatiable appetite for travel provides the richest crop of own goals.

In March 1971, Mr Jose Cayatania alighted at Heathrow Airport, London, in tropical gear and carrying a box of chocolates. 'Ah, nice to be in Tokyo,' he told perplexed airline staff. Mr C. was on his way from Los Angeles to Manila – but he chose the wrong departure gate.

The crowds turned out in Sicily in March 1980 to welcome the team from the English Second Division. There were TV cameras, the match was live on radio, an extra grandstand had been erected, and armed police stood by to curb any hot-headed supporters. The Sicilians were 'over the moon' when they won 3–1, and celebrated heartily. Then all was revealed. This wasn't Birmingham or Leicester City. They had been playing a team from the Second Division of the Lichfield and District Sunday Morning League.

There are own goals, as they say, in many fields. So perhaps we might discreetly raise the subject of sex. There was the strange case of the Family Planning Association who, according to their annual report in June 1971, set out to do a survey about virgins and non-virgins. But they couldn't find any virgins.

The sex urge can land people in hot water. Literally, in the case of the Scandinavian couple who made love on the pavement of a Florence street only to be doused with buckets by outraged housewives.

They moved on . . . to the middle of the street. This time someone turned a hosepipe on them.

They moved again . . . only to be hustled away in a police van. Police described the incident as 'man and woman overcome by intense heatwave'.

Some in the business world are occasionally overcome, too. In Germany, when a washing powder called Dash (known and loved in Britain as Daz) ran an advertising campaign quoting housewives as saying: 'I wouldn't swap my packet of Dash for two of another make,' they had an unexpected response. Hundreds of housewives contacted Dash saying they would like to make the deal. One person even tried to persuade them that, to live up to their ads, they were honour-bound to swap him one ton of Dash for two tons of Persil.

Then there was the Parker pen company, who promised customers they could 'prevent embarrassment' with an ink that didn't leak. In Mexico there was a slight mistranslation. 'Embarrassment' emerged as 'embarazar', altering the meaning to 'prevent pregnancy'. Parker were besieged by people who thought they had invented a wonder contraceptive.

Also putting their foot in it: a York shoe shop thought they had the perfect answer to pilferers with an outside display of all-right footwear. They hadn't bargained on a 43-year-old one-legged artist called Thomas Morris, who happily helped himself. He was only prevented from 'hopping it' by an alert store detective.

Other 'professionals' have been known to put the odd foot wrong.

Albert Einstein, mathematical genius, had a row with a conductor on the top of a London bus about his change. He later admitted he was in the wrong.

'Aerial flight is one of that class of problems with which man cannot cope,' declared US astronomer Simon Newcombe in 1903, when the Wright brothers were just taking to the air.

And Astronomer-Royal Sir Richard Woolley may have re-gretted his words in 1956: 'Space travel is utter bilge.'

That, you might say, is show business. Though those in the entertainment world can easily match the men of science. When an outrageous new pop star called Boy George first cruised into the charts with a song called 'Do you really want to hurt me?' even his peers were bemused. According to John Blake in *The Sun*, Rolling Stone Ronnie Wood wanted to know who the exciting new girl singer was – and tried to fix a date.

The manager of New York's famed Copacabana Club told a girl newcomer called Goldie Hawn: 'You aren't sexy enough.'

Critic John Horn of the now-defunct *New York Herald Tribune* said of a TV superstar-to-be: 'Johnny Carson has no apparent gift for the performing arts.'

And starlet Britt Ekland predicted in June 1976 of her new love, Rod Stewart: 'We'll be together for ever. We are like twins.'

Though one of the best recent showbiz boners came from Leslie Halliwell, chief film buyer for the ITV network. Turning down a chance to buy a TV show designed to challenge the supremacy of *Dallas* in April 1981, he said: 'When we actually viewed the programme our hearts sank. It is just an imitation, and a poor one at that.'

Mr Halliwell described the BBC's decision to take the show as 'verging on the paranoic'. Said Kit Miller, TV writer for *The Sun*: 'It could be the biggest British oil disaster since the Torrey Canyon.'

The show was called *Dynasty*, and within weeks it had knocked *Dallas* for six. It soon won more than 17 million British viewers, and at the height of its popularity one of its stars, Joan Collins, was clocking up 12 000 fan letters a week.

Sport, though, is the natural home of the own-goal. How often has one man's error altered the outcome of a major event, lost thousands of pounds of prize money, ruled out a winning certainty at the very last hurdle.

There was Lester Piggott, who turned down what proved to be the winning ride, All Along, in the 1983 Prix de L'Arc de Triomphe. Lester's chosen mount, Awaasif, came nowhere.

Roberto de Vicenzo, who lost the 1969 US Masters by signing an incorrectly-completed scorecard.

Finally there was Howard Chard the boxer and his match with Lee Oma in 1949. When the bell opened the first round, Chard started coughing and found he couldn't stop. He coughed so hard he had to sit down – and was counted out without receiving a single punch.

But 'own goal' inevitably conjures up a vision of the soccer pitch. And the medal for the most impressive of so many super own goals must surely go to Willie Donachie of Scotland.

Against Wales at Hampden in 1969, Donachie scored an own goal in majestic style, as the sportswriters say, quite out of nothing. Goalkeeper Jim Blyth threw out to Donachie to start a Scotland attack. The Scottish full-back never hesitated. He hit a first time left-foot drive straight for the goal. It thundered in just inside the near-post, with the goalkeeper nowhere. Donachie had equalised for Wales and the score stuck at 1–1.

Said *Daily Mail* soccer writer Jeff Powell: 'Had Blyth been expecting a shot from an opposing forward he might have saved. But as it was, he was as paralysed with astonishment as the rest of us.'

Well, at least that gave the sports commentators a field day. It isn't always so. These are the people whose snap pronouncements so often go wrong. To the delight of their public.

There was the woman tennis reporter who told how Martina Navratilova had won 'in straight sex'.

Another tennis buff, the BBC's Rex Alston, who declared: 'Louise Brough cannot serve at the moment because she has not got any balls.'

And John Oaksey, ITV racing commentator, who, describing a new concrete stand at York racecourse, said: 'Let's have a look at Major Petch's latest erection.'

That is not to say it doesn't happen to presenters, chat show hosts, newsmen and newswomen:

Johnny Carson once introduced comedienne Shari Lewis: 'And now a girl who is one of the bust peppiteers in the business.'

The BBC's Angela Rippon managed to talk of the government's 'gay pipelines' instead of 'pay guidelines'.

While fellow newsgirl Moira Stewart announced: 'There was heaving bombing today in the Southern Titty of Sidon.'

And let's not forget the weatherman who, noticing that a piece of his chart had dropped to the floor and the map behind him read 'Mist and og,' apologised: 'I'm sorry about the 'eff' in fog.'

On a more sombre note, death itself is the ultimate own goal.

On 15 April 1912, a Marconi operator joked with his colleague John Phillips on hearing of an emergency alert on the 'unsinkable' *Titanic*: 'Why not send out this new call, SOS – it might be your last chance to send it.' He was, unfortunately, quite right.

A 78-year-old grandmother emigrated to New Zealand from her native Belfast in 1970, telling her neighbours: 'I want to avoid all this street violence.' She died two years later from head injuries after she was hit by a placard during an Irish civil rights march.

If anyone should be able to see trouble coming, surely it is the army of stargazers and seers who minister to our thirst for knowing the future?

One such clairvoyant was Simon Alexander, of Worksop, Notts., who swept to international fame in the 1970s. Among his predictions for 1974 were that Ali would beat Frazier; Prince Charles would become engaged; it would be a record year for sunshine, and a good year for English cricket and Elizabeth Taylor. 'I am sure some of my predictions are right, it is just that I got the year wrong,' said Alexander later.

For 1975 he erroneously forecast President Ford would resign because of his wife's ill-health, Rudolph Hess would be freed on his 81st birthday and life would be discovered on another planet.

Unfortunately Mr Alexander was rather bad too at forecasting his own future and didn't foresee that it would be crossed by a tall dark stranger . . . the income tax man. In October, 1977, he appeared at a bankruptcy hearing in Chesterfield, Derbyshire, admitting debts of £17,000. The court heard that the clairvoyant unfortunately could not see the way clear to paying his bills.

This is, as we have said, a whole world of own-goals. There was the Australian woman, too embarrassed to give her name, who drove down a coal mine. She took a wrong turn off a mountain road from Melbourne to Sydney and thought she was in a tunnel. What made it worse was that she refused to give up, following the winding passage for five hours in all, demolishing the odd pit prop on the way. Her journey to the centre of the earth only came to an end when she finally ran out of petrol.

American writer Mrs Clare Boothe Luce came to grief when she failed to be patient with a hotel receptionist. 'What is your name, please, Madame,' asked one of the hotel staff. 'Look at the luggage,' Mrs Luce snapped.

The next morning she found her name in the hotel register as Miss Genuine Rawhide.

After ferociously growling at strangers for three years, guard dog Ben the golden labrador had his first big test when burglars broke into his owners' Northampton home in June, 1983. Unfortunately he sat meekly by while the raiders helped themselves to £1000 worth of cash and jewellery.

Ben made up for his inaction later though. He attacked the policemen who came to investigate the crime.

In July 1983, the ninety lifeboatmen of Harwich took their wives and friends on a pleasure cruise on the River Stour. Their boat ran aground and they had to be rescued . . . by the Harwich lifeboat.

12   Great Own Goals of History

1   DEATH OF JULIUS CAESAR, 44 BC

He had been behaving rather oddly for some time (wearing long red kinky boots, saying he was descended from a long line of ancient Alban kings, and getting himself made *dictator perpetuus*). But there was never a murder victim who walked so blithely to his fate. The prophetess Spurinna told him 'beware the Ides of March.' His wife Calpurnia begged him not to go to the Senate, she had had terrible dreams about it. He ignored a note pressed into his hands warning him of the plot.

At the pre-Ides supper, Caesar lifted a glass of wine and said he would prefer 'a sudden death'. He dreamed of shaking hands with Jupiter. He even dismissed his Spanish bodyguard. On the way to the Senate, he mocked Spurinna that the Ides had come and he was still not assassinated. Once there, he was surrounded by twelve conspirators led by Cassius and Brutus and stabbed twenty-three times.

Moral: *If you're warned to beware, 'ide somewhere.*

2   THE SPANISH ARMADA, 1588

The 'Invincible Armada' to give it its full title, was Philip II of Spain's futile attempt to overthrow Elizabeth I, with French help, and bring about an all-Catholic Europe. To do it, he sent 130 ships weighed down with 27 000 men, innumerable 50 pound cannons, and led by the inept Duque de Medina Sidonia, who knew nothing about the sea. First Drake set back the plan by 'singeing the King's beard' with forays at Cadiz and off Portugal. Next the Armada was kept from crossing the channel for two months by storms, sickness, and rotten stores. When the Spanish fleet did eventually blunder up the Channel poor tactics ruined its chance of pinning the English navy in harbour.

There were a few indecisive skirmishes before disaster at Calais. The French weren't ready to help the Spanish invade. Six English fireships were sent in and scattered the Armada northwards. The oversize ships limped home via the north of Scotland and Ireland. Many were wrecked on the rocks. Others were hit by typhoid. The Spaniards lost 51 ships with countless thousands dead; the English, no ships and barely a hundred men.

Moral: *Try 'arda and you'll come to less 'arm.*

3 NAPOLEON AT WATERLOO, 1815
Not until lunchtime, Josephine! Otherwise well-placed, Napoleon made a major blunder by delaying the start of his attack on the Duke of Wellington from morning until early afternoon. This allowed the ground to dry out and 45 000 Prussians, under Gen. Gebhard Von Blücher, to rally to the Iron Duke's side. When the French did eventually break through the English lines, leaving Wellington vulnerable, Napoleon was preoccupied with the Prussian threat to his flank and failed to press home his advantage. He lost 25 000 killed and wounded, with 9000 French taken prisoner. Four days later the emperor was forced to abdicate.

Moral: *Strike while the iron's hot – or be prepared to meet your Waterloo.*

4 BRITISH RETREAT FROM KABUL, 1842
In this incredible own goal in the first Afghan war, 4500 British troops and 12 000 civilians managed to get themselves wiped out by a handful of Afghan tribesmen. Pinned inside their camp on the outskirts of Kabul (they had inconveniently situated their stores ¼ mile away) the British under Gen. William Elphinstone

prematurely surrendered, believing they would be granted a safe trip home. This turned out to be an epic trek towards Jalalabad without even rudimentary reconnaissance. Without food, firewood, or shelter, many perished in the snow; others died from disease, or were casually picked off by the rebels. Finally soldiers on duty at the British fort at Jalalabad saw a lone ragged horseman riding towards them. He was a surgeon named Dr Brydon, the only European to survive the journey.

Moral: *If in doubt, carry on camping.*

5   CHARGE OF THE LIGHT BRIGADE, 1853
Into the valley of death. . . . Of 673 cavalrymen who made a suicide attack on heavy Russian guns at the battle of Balaclava, only 100 returned. The famous mass hara-kiri was the result of personal enmity between commanders Lord Lucan and Lord Cardigan who refused to use their commonsense after ambiguous orders from their superior, Lord Raglan. Rather like Dunkirk later, the ignominy was celebrated as glorious heroism when in reality it was a monster own goal.

Moral: *If in doubt don't just carry on regardless: stop and ask directions.*

6   CUSTER'S LAST STAND, 1876
General Custer's small 7th cavalry force was sent to punish Indians who had been raiding settlers and gold prospectors in the Black Hills of southern Montana. But on crossing the Little Bighorn River the famous long-haired, goatee general was confronted by Big Chief Sitting Bull's 1500 warrior braves. Custer split his 215 men into five companies, and little is known of the rest except that they were wiped out to the last man – thus earning, like the Light Brigade, their heroic place in history. Some say they were the bravest of the brave. Others that they were suffering from too much drink and sun. The General seemed to have an inkling something might happen. Just before the battle, he took out more than $5000 of life insurance.

Moral: *Only John Wayne could play John Wayne (and he was able to get up again afterwards).*

7 THE MAGINOT LINE, 1940

Named after its creator, War Minister André Maginot, and begun in 1929, the 'line' was an elaborate system of interlinked fortifications including bunkers, hidden gun emplacements, forts, and support positions – all pointing eastwards, towards Germany. By 1941 the Maginot Line had become a sick joke. When the Germans threatened to attack France in 1940, General Gamelin, the C-in-C, kept his entire army locked behind it. Even when the Germans began their Blitzkrieg through Belgium, Gamelin refused to see the warning signs, declaring this was merely a diversionary blind. The result was predictable. The Maginot Line did not extend to the Franco-Belgian border, and Hitler's men swept through the Lowlands into France, almost without resistance.

Moral: *Beware: trouble is always just round the corner.*

8 THE GERMAN ADVANCE ON MOSCOW, 1941

Hitler's foolhardy insistence on fighting on more than one front so he could win the war by the end of 1941 led to a major turning point in world history when his 'invincible' forces – three armies of 186 divisions – were destroyed trying to advance on Moscow. The German High Command had equipped the troops poorly and there was a total lack of winter clothing, despite temperatures down to $-40°$C. A whole host of diseases including typhoid devastated Hitler's Aryan supermen. In December 1941, 51 German divisions were driven back by a Soviet counter-attack and the war had reached its turning point.

Moral: *Don't fight on more than one front* and *always pack your winter woollies.*

9 SUEZ, 1956

Anthony Eden never recovered from this mammoth political banana-skin and Britain's credibility as a major world power slipped just as mightily. After President Nasser nationalized the largely British-owned Suez Canal, Britain and France joined the Israelis in military action against Egypt. After much huffing and puffing, British paratroopers went in, but world opinion – including both Russia and the US – was outraged. A UN cease-fire was agreed after superpower confrontation loomed; British troops returned tails between legs, and the Union Flag was left looking very tattered indeed.

Moral: *Where canals are concerned, do resist the temptation to drop in sometime.*

10 BAY OF PIGS, 1961

In April 1961, 1300 CIA-trained Cuban exiles mounted a comic opera attempt to overthrow Cuban dictator Fidel Castro. Transported in US merchant ships escorted by destroyers, all went well until the last minute, when President Kennedy denied them air cover. Poorly supported, landing at the wrong beach, and having to pick their way across swampland, they were easily routed by a large force of Cuban troops and militia.

Ninety of the invaders were killed and the rest taken prisoner in what was only part of a whole inglorious episode for US foreign policy. There were three attempts to poison Castro, all of which failed; a three-man assassination squad was sent, but failed to reach him. Finally, some CIA genius suggested germ warfare. The idea was that James Donovan, during negotiations to free the Bay of Pigs captives, should present Castro with a scuba diving suit contaminated on the inside with tuberculosis bacilli. Just for good measure it was dusted with a fungus to produce skin disease. All went well until Donovan, ignorant of the plan, gave Castro a clean, uncontaminated wet suit of his own.

Moral: *If you want to singe someone's beard, be sure you take enough firelighters.*

11 WATERGATE, 1972–74

By selecting dubious aides and condoning attempts by CREEP, the Committee for the Re-election of the President, to use dirty tricks to help him try and win every state in 1972, Richard Nixon found himself on the inexorable slide to ruin. Maintaining he had no part in a cover-up, he surrendered tapes of conversations in the White House. Eventually he was forced to release the recording for 23 June 1972 – the 'smoking gun' – in which he was heard ordering his men to block an FBI probe of the burglary at the Democratic HQ at the Watergate building. Nixon had been lying all along, and when in August 1974 impeachment seemed only a formality, he resigned from office – the first President to do so.

Moral: *Don't be a silly bug***, be content with 49 out of the 50 states plus the District of Columbia.*

12   THE IRAN HELICOPTER RESCUE, 1980
Caution and prevarication by President Carter led to the disaster in the desert at Tabas when six helicopters were sent from the 82nd airborne as part of the mission to rescue the 52 US Embassy hostages in Tehran. Carter had directed the operation throughout and had scaled it down in size from an initial 350 man force. This minimized possible casualties but greatly increased the chances of failure. After one of the helicopters took in sand and was written off, the mission was aborted. In the chaos that followed another helicopter careered into a C-130 transport plane. Eight men died, three more were badly burned. Carter gallantly accepted the blame, but his humiliation at Tabas coupled with his impotence at getting the hostages released helped Ronald Reagan to a big win just a few months later.

Moral: *You're in for a lot of bovver with insufficient hovver.*

2

I've Just Shot Myself in the Foot, or Life's Little Misfortunes

Coming a Cropper

The bandit was all nerves as, finger twitching on the trigger, he pointed his sub-machine gun at the pop star's head. 'Drive, or I'll blow your head off,' he said somewhat discouragingly to Tony Price of *Revolver*.

Mr Price did as he was told. He drove – straight into a pile of deep sand. Whereupon the highly agitated highwayman made the biggest blunder in the armed robber's handbook . . . *he shot himself in the foot*.

Said Mr Price, of Finchley, London, who was holidaying in Israel in October 1969 with his group: 'I grabbed his gun, hurled it out of the car, then we gave him a hefty shove in the backside out of the door. He limped off into the dunes, but police were able to catch up with him by following the trail of blood.'

George Gibson of Knoxville, Tennessee reached for a cigarette, put it in his mouth, and lit it. It cured him of smoking. It wasn't a ciagarette he lit – it was a firework.

When a Swiss chef lost a finger in a meat-slicing machine, he put in an insurance claim. The company thought the chef might have been at fault so they sent along an investigator to test the machine. The insurance man, too, lost a finger. The chef's claim was approved.

A weekly magazine swore this was true: At the Royal Tournament in Earls Court, London, an ammunition case fell 60 feet from a makeshift 'cliff' being scaled by a team from the Royal Marines, hitting a sergeant-major on the head. The sergeant-major was only dazed. The ammo box was a write-off.

Alfred Zuhl of Michigan holds the amazing distinction of being eaten whole by a vacuum cleaner. The hungry Hoover was in fact, a large industrial street cleaner. Poor Alfred, aged 11, was cycling round it when he skidded, fell . . . and was sucked up inside the machine, complete with bike. A squad of mechanics dismantled the beast and out walked Alfred, suffering only bruises and shock. His first words on being freed: 'Where's my cap?'

When Brian Clements of Slough, Berks., rang the fire brigade to tell them about another bizarre accident in 1976, there were guffaws all round. Mr Clements told them his wife had become anchored to the mattress by a spring which had popped out and ensnared a delicate part of her anatomy. The date . . . April 1.

'You don't expect us to fall for that one,' laughed the firemen. Unfortunately it was all quite true.

When Mr Clements did manage to persuade them of his wife's predicament, it took six firemen, three ambulancemen and a doctor to free her.

A fire brigade spokesman said: 'We really do owe Mrs Clements an apology. We did think it was an April Fool's joke.'

Some people are born unlucky. Take M. Baenard Acheriaux, a 38-year-old shopkeeper from Puy, in Auvergne. He was dubbed 'the unluckiest man in France' after suffering 28 disasters, not one of them his fault.

First, in September 1980, the river Loire burst its banks, flooding several acres of his woodland. Then his car was struck by another while parked by the side of the road. A few weeks later the car caught fire, before being stolen no less than four times. Each time it was returned even more badly damaged.

M. Acheriaux bought a cement mixer to do repairs to his house, but it was crushed by a car whose owner had lost control. Twice, a lorry dumped its entire load on his bonnet.

Even his billiard table was written off after being dropped by a removal firm. Though he didn't need it at the time — he had just suffered his fourteenth bone fracture while playing rugby.

Later his chimney and part of his roof were blown off. A professor committed suicide in the cellar of his shop. And much of his woodland was destroyed by fire.

Said M. Acheriaux: 'From now on, when I see a ladder or black cat I'll cross to the other side of the road. One can't be too careful.'

It is to be hoped he didn't take up Break Dancing. This craze for doing mind-boggling leaps, spins, jumps and splits to pounding disco music, which reached its height in 1984, lived up quite literally to its name with some heavy new business for hospital orthopaedic units. In the first months of Break Dancing, US hospitals reported one man left a quadriplegic and nine others with serious injuries. Efrain Arreola, 25, an accountant from Mexico City, broke his neck while Break Dancing near Chicago's Lakefront.

A Soviet housewife, Alexander Lopatina, used her rolling pin one day in 1984 to weigh down a pan of boiling potatoes. She got more than she bargained for. There was a massive explosion and her kitchen was wrecked. What she had used as a 'rolling pin' was in fact a second world war German mine.

Paul Robinson, 19, of Woking, Surrey, was swept away by strong currents at Littlehampton, Sussex, in September 1983,

after going for a midnight swim. Lifeboatmen found him cling-
ing to a sign saying: 'No swimming'.

Few can beat the record of young bride Sue Taylor, 17, of
Scunthorpe. She was rushed to hospital from her wedding
reception in April 1978 after tripping over the train of her
flowing white wedding gown, and breaking her arm.

What made it worse was the guests thought it was all part of
the celebrations. As she lay writhing on the floor in agony, the
60 guests just laughed. 'We thought she was joking,' explained
mother-in-law Mrs Olive Bates.

Said Sue: 'It's not every girl who turns up at hospital in her
wedding gown.'

An own goal to please every schoolboy was scored by angry dad
Tom Jeffries of Dersingham, Norfolk. He spanked his son
Stephen, 5, and promptly dislocated his own arm. The punishment . . . an anaesthetic while his shoulder was reset, and a
fortnight off work. Doctors told him: 'Dislocate it again and it
means an operation.' Mrs Jeffries said: 'It definitely hurt him
more than it hurt Stephen.'

Another man who had to live through the pain barrier was the
Japanese official who bowed so low when the carriage of
Emperor Hirohito came to a stop, he cracked his head on the
door as it opened. The Emperor was a model of decorum. When
the official's head had been bandaged, he made him bow again.

Then there was New York policeman Clive Parsons. In the summer of 1983, worried his girlfriend needed some protection from all those muggers and rapists, he brought her a spray can of knock-out gas.

Preparing for a date with her that very evening, he showered and shaved at the Precinct, put on a clean shirt and reached for what he thought was his can of hair oil.

It was the gas. He awoke next morning in hospital.

Finally, in June 1970, the *Daily Mail* told of this unfortunate chain of own goals to a man who had just moved into a new house in Johannesburg.

Awakened by the burglar alarm, he grabbed his revolver, leaped out of bed – but the house being new to him, ran through a glass partition separating the lounge from the dining room. He was taken to hospital suffering from cuts. Meanwhile, his wife set about clearing up the mess. Finding that water would not remove the bloodstains from the floor, she cleaned up with petrol. She then disposed of the petrol down the lavatory, forgetting, however, to pull the flush.

Her stitched and bandaged husband was soon returned to her. But seeking to soothe his nerves, he retired to the lavatory and lit a cigar.

A mistake. Instantly there was an explosion, followed by a sheet of flame. After dragging out her dazed and charred

husband, the lady called an ambulance for the second time. They came, but on their way out in the dark, lost their bearings and fell headlong over the rockery.

The stitched, bandaged, charred and dazed husband was tipped ingloriously on to the rocks – breaking his collar bone.

Chronic Misjudgment

Before the Guyana massacre and all that poisoned Kool-Aid, a California State Congressman waxed lyrical about the preacher who had so many other people's interest at heart: 'San Francisco should have ten more Rev. Jim Joneses,' said Rep. Willie Brown.

'I'll tell you, Lyndon, the Vice-Presidency isn't worth a pitcher of warm spit,' said one-time Democratic choice for the ticket, John Nance Garner.

'I have the last say in everything with Liz now,' said Richard Burton in 1964.

This is the chapter of chronic misjudgment. Supergoof. Where they've got it all wrong – in one.

> 'At the opera saw *Romeo and Juliet* (Shakespeare) the first time it was ever acted, a play that is the worst I ever saw in my life. *Midsummer Night's Dream* (Shakespeare) which I had never seen before, nor shall never again, for it is the most insipid, ridiculous play I ever saw in my life.
> . . . Saw *Twelfth Night* (Shakespeare) a silly play, and not related at all to the name or day.'
> *Samuel Pepys, Diaries 1662/3*

Ayatollah Khomeini will one day be viewed as some kind of saint.
Andrew Young, US Ambassador to the UN, 1976

He falls instantly in and out of love. His present attachment will follow the course of all the others.
Winston Churchill on Edward VIII and Mrs Simpson

What will she call herself? Queen of England of course. And Empress of India – the whole bag of tricks.

Edward VIII on Mrs Simpson

I don't think there'll be a war. The Führer doesn't want his new buildings bombed.

Unity Mitford, 1938

I cannot conceive of any condition which would cause this ship to founder. I cannot conceive of any vital disaster happening to this vessel. Modern shipbuilding has gone beyond that.

E. J. Smith, Captain of the Titanic

Biggs, it is my unpleasant duty to inform you that your earliest possible release date is 12 January 1984.

Governor of Lincoln Jail to a new inmate, train robber Ronald Biggs, in 1964

(He managed to get out a bit earlier than that)

Q. Are you alarmed or concerned? Does this unrest present a threat to internal stability or to the regime?
A. No, not at all.

Shah of Iran, 1978

He was completely lovable to every individual while working for me. Never was there any deviation from the highest proper sense of things.

S. Russell Blomerth, employer of Albert De Salvo – the Boston Strangler

A third rate burglary attempt not worthy of further White House comment.

Ron Ziegler, White House press spokesman on the Watergate break-in, 19 June 1972

I've got what it takes to stay.

Richard Nixon, November 1973

A Toast to Lady Jane

At a lunch for 200 civic heads and industrialists in February 1981, Scottish business doyen Peter Balfour wished Prince Charles all the best with his bride to be. Unfortunately he toasted the Prince's future happiness and long-life partnership with . . . 'Lady Jane'.

Ivor Spencer, president of the Guild of Professional Toastmasters, tells how he heard the chairman at a plush city luncheon welcome the Queen Mother to 'this hysterical occasion' and another turn to Prince Philip and say: 'It's a great honour for you to come here and dine with us.'

These are the own goals all those in the public eye fear. Super bloopers. Stultifying gaffes. Monstrous clangers before huge or distinguished audiences.

Even experienced talkers can end up red-faced. Roy Jenkins, addressing the inmates of a London jail, started his speech with the words: 'How nice to see you all here.' While Denis Thatcher managed to introduce prisoners' chum Lord Longford as the fugitive Lord *Lucan*.

It's an occupational hazard for politicians, of course. In August 1983, Roy Hattersley tried to woo left-wing Labour support with an impassioned speech against the class structure and racism. All went well until he took questions from the audience. He was asked: 'Is it right to openly refer to race and racism?' In reply Mr Hattersley said: 'I believe in calling a spade a spade.' As the audience laughed, Mr Hattersley turned bright pink. His questioner said: 'Someone might report you if you did.'

It goes right up to the top, of course. Mrs Thatcher caused pressmen to fall about when, presenting a retirement present to a journalist, she recalled how 'he met his wife on the job'. She repeated the *double entendre* on a TV chat show with Michael Aspel in July 1984, telling fellow guest Barry Manilow, to his total bemusement: 'I'm always on the job.'

President Reagan got himself into a little local difficulty in 1984 when President and Mrs Mitterrand of France paid a State visit to Washington.

Mr Reagan speaking no French and Mrs Mitterrand having no English, they had a slight communication problem as they walked arm in arm to a formal dinner.

Suddenly Mrs Mitterrand stopped abruptly. Said the President later: 'She calmly turned her head and said something to me in French, which unfortunately I did not understand.'

There was then something of a French farce as the butler motioned to the pair to come forward, Mrs Mitterrand refused, Mr Reagan tried to urge her on, and she repeated her objections in her native tongue.

Finally an interpreter lost in the rush, appeared and, gently as he could, translated for the President. He explained that Mrs Mitterrand was saying: 'I can't move. You are standing on my gown.'

Then there was the amorous French skipper who turned up at the bar on a Caribbean island rather the worse for drink. A rather smart-looking lady took his eye, and, not wanting to waste words, he went over straight away and tried to sit on her lap. He was immediately hustled away. The island was Mustique and he had been trying to plonk himself on a knee that was hardly used to such intrusion. It belonged to Princess Margaret.

With some members of the Royal Family the boot is usually on the other foot. The Duke of Edinburgh, in particular, has also enjoyed a reputation as prince of the faux-pas. During Britain's little local difficulty with Argentina, in May 1982 Prince Philip gave a speech condemning all conflicts as 'stupid and unnecessary'. Buckingham Palace hurriedly issued a statement saying he was not, of course, referring to the Falklands.

Show business has produced many a lofty gaffe. The late David Niven used to tell how he dressed up as a clown for a high society fancy dress ball. Then a young army officer, he thought the butler looked at him a bit strangely when he turned up in thick make up, false nose, and carrying a pound of sausages.

But the drawing room door opened and he was announced to the gathering in traditional style. Then the full horror struck him. The room was packed with notables – all in immaculate evening dress. The future film star had turned up at the right place – but on the wrong date.

They weren't even grateful for the sausages.

Prominent Hollywood producer Ray Stark told how he scored against himself in the noblest of company. At a formal reception at a stately home in England, he and his wife were approached by a servant in tails who inquired politely: 'And what is yours?'

Mr Stark thought he was a waiter and replied: 'Two Bloody Marys.' The man spun on his heels, walked to the head of the stairs and announced loudly: 'Mr and Mrs Bloody Mary.'

Poor Selina Scott is to British television what the Duke of Edinburgh is to the Royal Family. At a star-studded ITV spectacular in 1982 to salute the Falklands task force, she introduced Richard Todd as Sir John Mills, Denholm Elliott as Donald Sinden, and managed to confuse Virginia McKenna with Dame Anna Neagle.

Later she uttered an unladylike four letter word on the BBC's *Breakfast Time* show, and managed to let slip to thousands of watching toddlers that there was no such person as Father Christmas.

Of the four letter word she said: 'I didn't realise the mike was open. I felt dreadful afterwards.'

An American radio reporter covering the June 1984 D-Day commemoration was assigned to cover the arrival of the Royal Yacht Britannia, and began to wax lyrical.

'And here she comes, sailing across the calm waters of the British Channel. Majestic and regal, a ship truly fit for a Queen.'

At that point someone pointed out he was, in fact, not describing Her Majesty's yacht. He had gone into raptures about a Townsend Thoresen car ferry.

Broadcasting is a competitive game, of course, and Radio 4's *Today* programme was brought to a temporary halt in June, 1983 when presenter John Timpson threw a ball to colleague Peter Hobday he just could not handle.

Retired Royal Navy officer Captain Sam Lombard-Hobson had been recalling the days when society dances were held aboard ship. 'All those magnificent balls on deck,' he mused.

After the item linkman Timpson, handing over to Hobday, remarked: 'Ah, how well I remember those magnificent balls on deck.'

Thirty seconds of silence followed as Hobday tried to regain his composure. All the listeners heard were moans, coughs, and some half-suppressed shrieks. The BBC said: 'It was just one of those things that sometimes happen.'

Certain words do bring out the guffaws. During the Desert Classic golf tournament in Palm Springs, Bob Hope was joking for the TV cameras with an attractive young scorekeeper.

'How old are you?' he asked.

'Twenty four,' she answered.

'My, I've got balls older than you,' quipped the comedian, before realising what he had said and almost choking with embarrassment.

American television host Dick Cavett once fronted an early morning show on ABC called *This Morning*. One day among his guests was transexual Christine Jorgensen.

She told him: 'Sex is not determined by genitals alone.'

He leaned forward and said: 'I don't think I quite grasp that.'

Those responsible for the printed word don't escape either. In October 1983 Cabinet Minister Cecil Parkinson resigned because his secretary, Miss Sarah Keays, was expecting his child – something of an epic own goal in itself. The same month his Department of Trade and Industry published a magazine, *British Business* with a cover showing a stork arriving with a natal bundle in its beak. The headline: 'Facts of Life.'

An Australian charity booking boomeranged on down-under entertainer Rolf Harris. He thought he was appearing at a 'do' staged by estate agents Hookers in his home town of Perth.

When he got there he realised that the 'Hookers' Ball' was, well, just that. The city's prostitutes had arranged the 100-dollar-a-plate function at a top hotel to raise money for children's charities. Mr Harris was reported to be 'somewhat brassed off'.

Finally, two Danish football fans were suitably caught on the rebound when they were out celebrating their country's shock defeat of England at Wembley in September 1983.

Two Englishmen, in deep gloom over the defeat, had the bad luck to be caught up with a party from Copenhagen who were staying at their hotel in Regent's Park. The Danes taunted them.

OK, said one of the Englishmen, businessman David Roberts, perhaps you'd like to accept a sporting challenge yourselves. A quarter of a mile race round the park, perhaps?

The confident Danes accepted and selected their two best men to take on the English. To their surprise, they were trounced in dramatic style.

Mr Roberts's companion – the man who won the race – was no also-ran. They had taken on Steve Cram, world champion at 1500 metres.

12 Top Gaffes by Anchormen, Newscasters and Presenters

1 You are now going to hear the bum of the flightelbee.

Stuart Hibberd, first BBC radio
announcer (attrib.)

2 Ah, the Queen has just left the bridge of HMS Vanguard and has gone down below for some reason or other . . . (*long pause*) . . . and now I can see water coming through the side of the ship . . .

John Snagge, stuck for something to
say on King and Queen's visit to
Canada, 1939

3 Stay tuned for Charles Dickens's immortal classic 'A Sale of Two Titties'.

US station announcer

4 I miss the thrill of riding and the sound of those hounding pooves.

Jimmy Edwards, TV interview

5   This is the British Broadcorping Castration.
>
> *BBC announcer*

6   There she is, the huge vast bulk of her.
>
> *Wynford Vaughan-Thomas, BBC, to*
> *a close-up of HRH the Queen Mother*
> *during the launching of the* Ark Royal

7   Rolls-Royce announced today that it is recalling all Rolls-Royce cars made after 1966 because of faulty nuts behind the steering wheels.
>
> *Walter Cronkite, famed US*
> *anchorman*

8   Ladies and gentlemen, Mr Eddie Playbody will now pee for you.
>
> *US linkman introducing the banjoist*

9   A squid as you know, of course, has ten testicles.
>
> *Graham Kerr, 'The Galloping*
> *Gourmet'*

10   Goods are shitting on the supermarket selves.
>
> *Sue Lloyd-Roberts, ITN*

11   The play tells of a man haunted by a faint queer.
>
> *David Hamilton, ATV* (he meant
> 'quaint fear')

12   President Carter has painful haemorrhoids and is being treated by his physician, Rear Admiral ... William Lookass ... Lukash ... ?
>
> *US newscaster*

30 Ways to Avoid Disaster and Distress at Parties

1   DON'T try to be the first to arrive ... you'll end up being saddled with the most boring people at the party.

2 DON'T be the last to leave . . . you'll end up being saddled with the most boring people at the party.

3 DON'T forget to check whether the party is fancy dress . . . if it *is* and you *aren't* you'll feel a fool; if it *isn't* and you *are* you'll look a complete idiot.

4 DON'T say 'Hi, Cynth' if you can't remember the name of your hostess. Just say 'Great to see you,' put your head down, and make for the bar.

5 DON'T make fun of other people's garb. The man with the fancy waistcoat, funny hat and sash is probably an ambassador or rear admiral.

6 DON'T say to a priest 'I like your frock.' He's heard it a thousand times and didn't think it was funny in the first place.

7 DON'T, on board ship, say to the Captain 'Who's driving?' Likewise, he's heard it a thousand times and didn't think it was funny to start with.

8 DON'T forget to look at the carpet. If it's dark, you're OK to spill red wine over it. If it's light, or worst of all,

white, make sure you stick to white wine, gin or vodka.

9   DON'T say to anyone you don't like the chintz curtains or the psychedelic colour scheme. You'll find you have been talking to the hostess's sister/hostess's mother/the host.

10 DON'T say to a stranger you fancy the blond(e) in the corner, she/he looks as if she/he might do a turn. It will be his/her live-in lover, sister, or oldest friend.

11 DON'T talk about politics, football, or Christianity, or you are positively inviting people to bore you to tears out of revenge. Preferred subjects: astrology, Zen Buddhism, Laura Ashley prints, reincarnation, ceramics.

12 DON'T criticize the record collection too loudly. Someone has to like Mantovani and the King Singers – probably the host and hostess.

13 DON'T position yourself too near the bar (you'll be trampled underfoot *and* drink will be spilled all over you), or too far from the food.

14 DON'T get too excited in the food queue. One elbow is quite sufficient. Two unfortunately invites swift and painful retaliation.

15 DON'T draw attention to having too much ash by shouting 'Where are the ruddy ashtrays, then?' Take a cue from other smokers in the room . . . Wait until no one is looking and then stub your tab end out forcefully on the carpet.

16 DON'T forget to gen up on the latest buzz words, and where they come from: joint (butchers); tab (chemists); coke (NCB); snow (Eskimos); and Big H (Hull Kingston Rovers).

17   DON'T,while enjoying yourself, give anyone your name and address and invite them round the following weekend. They're sure to turn up.

18   DON'T try to sell anyone anything. To do so invites swift and terrible retribution, unless you want more double glazing or to join the Moonies.

19   DON'T if you feel queasy, make for the bathroom. There's sure to be somebody in there. Go straight outside.

20   DON'T volunteer to go to the off-licence for more booze. You'll end up having to pay for it.

21   DON'T volunteer to put a few records on. You'll end up being unpaid disc jockey for the night.

22   DON'T volunteer to do any washing up. You'll end up being unpaid dishwasher for the night.

23   DON'T be seen going into a bedroom with a member of the opposite sex (especially if their wife/husband/boyfriend/girlfriend is at the party too). The likelihood is that nothing will happen; but everyone else will assume that it has.

24   DON'T sit on laps before 0200.

25   DON'T wink at anyone after 0300.

26   DON'T make jokes about orgies or group sex . . . or they might surprise you and all suddenly take their clothes off.

27   DON'T forget to go carefully on your way out, watching particularly for low beams and high steps. More accidents occur to people leaving a party than to stunt men, jockeys, and do-it-yourself nuts put together.

28   DON'T give any of the late guests the merest hint of where you live, e.g. north, south, east, west. To do so is to invite being made to do a 20-mile detour to suit that practised reveller you've been trying to avoid all evening.

29   DON'T give any of the late guests the merest hint of any spare room, camp bed, sofa, sleeping bag, floor space – even that you have a bath or a garage. To do so is to invite three or four days' company from the practised reveller you've been trying to avoid all evening.

30   FINALLY, DON'T attach balloons, garlands, tickertape etc. to the outside of your car, or drive round in fancy hats, or in hire costume blowing whoopee whistles. To do so is to invite attendance at another sort of party, down at the local nick, with the other participants definitely not in fancy dress.

3

Always Try to Carry a Spare Pair of Trousers

Political Own Goals

'You're a man of the past. The future doesn't interest you,' Valéry Giscard d'Estaing taunted his rival, Francois Mitterrand, in a TV election debate in May, 1973.

'Nobody thought he'd go far at all,' said Miss Zuba Chiles, schoolteacher of Grandview, Missouri, on one of America's great presidents, Harry S. Truman.

Here a selection of political chickens that came home to roost – boomerangs which definitely did come back.

Somebody in the Democratic Party had a good idea. Instead of all the infighting and backbiting in the run-up to the 1984 election, the eight Democratic contenders would stop sniping at each other and jet together across the U.S. with a message of unity, raising hard cash. The $2.4 million 'purse' could then go to the campaign funds of the eventual winner.

Well, it seemed like a good idea. Jesse Jackson fired the first salvo, saying the rest of them weren't interested in minorities or the poor. Alan Cranston quarrelled with party chairman Charles Manatt, and refused to join the trip. And Reuben Askew cried off when his mother-in-law died.

At the first stop in Atlanta, Gary Hart accused John Glenn of being a closet Republican. Glenn accused Mondale of being a liberal spendthrift. In Chicago, there was a bitter public feud between party chiefs and mayor Harold Washington; a lunch in St Louis was cancelled through lack of interest; and at the final stop, Albuquerque, Ernest 'Fritz' Hollings declared the Glenn and Mondale campaigns were 'mush'.

At the close of the trip – described by those involved as 'merciful' – the tour had raised less than half its target, and the squabbles in the Democratic Party had surfaced for all to see.

Yes, it had seemed like a good idea.

But American political leaders have scored some spectacular own goals. There was US ambassador to the UN Warren Austin, who declared in 1948 during the Middle East war, that Arabs and Jews should get together and settle their differences 'like good Christians.'

There was US Secretary of State William Jennings Bryan, who invited land-locked Switzerland to send its navy to the opening of the Panama Canal.

As professional a figure as Senator Robert F. Kennedy 'blooped' during an otherwise triumphant tour of Africa. As he landed in Nairobi to be greeted by Kenyan government minister Tom Mboya, Kennedy was surrounded by a jaunty throng of Africans. He gave them a cheery 'thumbs up' signal. Of course, in much of the world that means OK, great, wonderful – but not in Kenya. It wasn't as bad as it might have been. But the Senator had just given his welcomers the campaign sign of the Kenyan Communist Party.

Few would let leading Republican John Connally forget his monster faux-pas in 1973. While attempting to speak in defence of the then under-fire Vice-president he said: 'I hope that Spiro Agnew will be completely exonerated and found guilty of the charges against him.'

Margaret Thatcher has been known to let the odd slip show. During a tour of Canada in September 1982, Mrs Thatcher upset more than a few people by failing to remember where she was. 'You too have difficulties with unemployment in the United States,' she confidently told an interviewer in Ottawa.

Neil Kinnock was propelled to the leadership of Britain's Labour Party in 1983 despite a small avalanche of own goals. He turned his car over on the M4 while on the way from a late night engagement, he lost his voice through too much windbag-ging. He arrived only fairly triumphant at the Brighton confer-ence to a row about using cars with non-union drivers. Then, posing happily for photographers, he managed to fall into the sea.

Accidents happen in the SDP too. Shirley Williams has gained an unenviable reputation over the years for being disorganised and rather daffy. She put paid to the stories with a categorical denial she had ever been late for a train.

Unfortunately, when the SDP joined with the Liberals to sail down the Thames in May 1984 on the 'Alliance Euro-boat', Shirley undid all the good work. The poster-bedecked barge waited half an hour in the full glare of TV cameras at Sonning, Berks, but without any hint of her whereabouts, decided to cast off without her.

The huffing, puffing Mrs Williams turned up minutes later. Oh dear, Shirley, they all said. Missed the boat again.

Not that Mrs Williams could claim to be anywhere near Britain's most foot-in-mouth politician. Making a strong chal-lenge for this honour in the 1983 Parliament was John Butcher, Conservative MP for Coventry South-West and a junior minis-ter at the Department of Trade and Industry.

He first came to prominence attempting to lose Mrs Thatcher millions of votes in November 1983 by calling Northerners 'workshy'. Both he and she were forced to apologise in the House of Commons. Then, in March 1984, he tried to offend his party's millions of churchgoing supporters by saying clergy-men should give up politics for Lent. Countered the Bishop of Coventry, the Right Rev. John Gibbs: 'Politics is too important to be left to politicians.'

In a single speech in June 1984 Mr Butcher managed to drop two clangers. First, he committed the Government to the creation of 750,000 new jobs, a figure which caused his boss, Employment Secretary Tom King, to simulate a bilious attack. Second, he managed to say of the Japanese: 'We can beat them in the 1980s and 1990s. We have beaten them in other respects and we can do it again.'

On the eve of the arrival of the Japanese Prime Minister for the London Economic Summit, this reference to 1945 was said to have been considered by the Prime Minister 'tactless in the extreme'.

Come on, Mr Butcher, chop chop!

That thought brings us neatly to the case of David Marston, US Attorney for Pennsylvania in the Carter years. He was a Republican who had upset leading local Democrats, though his loyalty was unquestioned.

So much so that when summoned to Washington in January 1978, during the worst snowstorm in years, he made superhuman efforts to get there.

All flights were cancelled, so Mr Marston rushed and caught a train. When this was derailed outside Baltimore, he was undaunted. He completed his journey by bus.

Finally, somewhat weary but pleased to have triumphed over the elements and demonstrated his dedication, he made it to the US Justice Department for his interview with the President.

Mr Carter told him: 'I didn't want to tell you this in a letter. You're fired.'

Relations between the powerful and the press are not always as they should be. *Washington Post* reporter Carl Bernstein telephoned John Mitchell in September, 1973, and informed him his newspaper would be running a story about him the next day. It would say that, while he was Attorney-General, Mitchell had controlled secret funds to finance covert intelligence-gathering from the Democrats.

Mitchell referred directly to the publisher of the paper. He told Bernstein: 'Kate Graham's gonna get her tit caught in a big fat wringer if that's published!'

The *Washington Post* did run the article – and John Mitchell's comment. It ruined him.

Perhaps one of the most celebrated political humblings came to then Chancellor of the Exchequer Sir Geoffrey Howe when, in November 1983, he lost his trousers on the overnight Manchester to London express.

The theft was a world-shattering incident. Even in Moscow they were stunned. Thundered *Komsomolskaya Pravda*, organ of the young communist league: 'He got out of a tricky situation because he had a spare pair of trousers, but the British people have had their trousers shortened by budget scissors and are unable to get out of their predicament.'

A few months later, Sir Geoffrey had trouble with his trousers again. This time he spilled coffee over them on a plane taking him to Bonn. A frantic search located his suitcase at the bottom of the plane's luggage hold, and a spare pair was recovered just in time to prevent him having to venture trouserless into talks with West German foreign minister Herr Genscher.

Sir Geoffrey's predecessor at the Foreign Office, Francis Pym, went one better. He managed to commit political hara-kiri on television in June 1983 by saying he wished the Tories wouldn't get too many votes in the election. A landslide would be a bad thing, he declared. Mr Pym's reward was not long in coming – three days after the poll he was unceremoniously dumped on the back benches.

In his later years always, it seemed, on the receiving end, was SDP leader Roy Jenkins. Campaigning in Hillhead, Glasgow during the by-election he won, he approached a Indian-looking voter and began his spiel.

'How long have you been here?' asked Woy.

'A lot longer than you,' was the instant reply to the electoral carpetbagger.

After the June 1983 election, the SDP fell far short of the targets they had set themselves, winning just six seats out of 150.

Woy made predictable noises, talking of the millions voting SDP and how it was now 'very much the start of a new chapter' for the party.

He was right. Three days later he was replaced by Dr David Owen.

Let's Go to the People

'They must find someone else . . . even if they can't agree on Rab or Quintin there must be someone else. But please, not me.' Hard luck. Enter in October 1963 Britain's most reluctant

Prime Minister, Sir Alec Douglas-Home.

'When we got into office, the thing that surprised me most was to find that things were just as bad as we'd been saying they were,' said John F. Kennedy in May 1961. Served him right.

'Let's go to the people. I'm happy and I believe you are,' said Labour Premier James Callaghan, launching his fatal re-election campaign in April 1979.

Some more political mis-shots.

> We have the momentum now, and I just know we are going to win.
>
> *Incumbent Gerald R. Ford,*
> *November 1976, four days before*
> *losing to Jimmy Carter*

> Our judgment is that the presence of the Royal Marines garrison . . . is sufficient deterrent against any possible aggression.
>
> *Prime Minister Margaret Thatcher, in*
> *a letter to Mrs Madge Nichols of*
> *Gerrard's Cross, February, 1982,*
> *wrongly predicting 48 marines could*
> *repel the entire Argentine military*

She should have listened to her own spokesmen.

> A display of weakness on the Falkland Islands is likely to precipitate precisely the kind of crisis we want to avoid.
>
> *Christopher Tugendhat, Conservative*
> *spokesman on foreign affairs,*
> *February 1976*

> The spirit of victory is in the air!
>
> *Hugh Gaitskell, Labour leader, on his*
> *way to a drubbing, October 1950*

> People think that what I expose is the whole. There are things that one passionately wants to keep private, things that are no one's business. What isn't realised is how professionally I don't expose what I don't want to.
>
> *Jeremy Thorpe, before the Norman*
> *Scott affair*

When I tell Dick Nixon what to do, he listens. I'm in charge.

> *John Mitchell, to Republican*
> *Congressmen, 1968*

What do these rumours amount to? They amount to the fact that a minister is said to be acquainted with a very pretty girl . . . I should have thought that was a matter for congratulation rather than inquiry.

> *Reginald Paget, Tory MP, on the*
> *Profumo affair, March 1963*

I do not think that anyone should believe the polls, because they often get it wrong.

> *Michael Foot, February 1983*

There is a strong, almost overwhelming probability that the Alliance will get more votes than Labour.

> *Roy Jenkins, June 1983*

I know I am going to be President.

> *Senator Gary Hart*

I Wish the Secretary of State Were Here . . .

'Ronald Reagan is perceived as a most conservative Republican,' said Gerald Ford after the 1980 New Hampshire primary. 'A very conservative Republican can't win in a national election.'

Mind you, he was the man who set up a committee called Constructive Republican Alternative Proposals – but everybody called them by their initials, CRAP.

Said Lyndon Johnson on Vietnam, in 1967: 'The enemy knows he has met his match in the field.'

American Presidents are known for, well, the odd goof.

If Ford and Carter had done plenty of groundwork, Ronald Reagan didn't disappoint the aficionados. In the early days he shambled through press conferences. He slept through international crises. He seemed blissfully unaware of everything that was going on.

He claimed in January 1982: 'There are a million more people working than a year ago.' Well, actually no. Half a million less.

He upset Buckingham Palace telling reporters he'd been invited to the Royal Wedding . . . when no invitations had gone out.

He upset the feminists when he said: 'I happen to believe if it weren't for women, us men would still be walking around in skin suits carrying clubs.'

When he was asked at a press conference in October 1982 about rival Greek and Turkish claims to Cyprus, he looked visibly stumped. 'Oh, I wish the Secretary of State were here,' he said languidly.

The November 1983 tour of the Far East showed how Mr Reagan could get his act totally untogether. In a speech to Japanese MPs, a friendly phrase he had rehearsed came out as a meaningless jumble. At a meal with Prime Minister Yasuhiro Nakasone, Mr Reagan and Nancy had to sit on the floor. They looked decidedly uncomfortable as their chopsticks flailed.

Next the President let slip an uncharacteristic swearword at a TV rehearsal. He said when he became President 'Our recession was 12 per cent' (he meant inflation). And finally he managed to talk of Cuba being 'in the Mediterranean'.

Yes, Mr Secretary, wish you were here.

The Presidency obviously didn't suit William Henry Harrison. In 1841 he became the 9th President of the USA, but caught a cold at his inauguration. He died just 31 days later, the shortest term on record.

Herbert Hoover lasted longer, but was even less successful in the job. Elected in 1928 to all sorts of promises about economic security, he presided three months later over the Wall Street Crash.

In retrospect, his election year words take some beating: 'We in America today are nearer the final triumph over poverty than anyone before in the history of any land . . . we have not yet reached the goal, but given a chance to go forward with the policies of the last eight years, we shall soon with the help of

God be in the sight of the day when poverty will be banished from this nation.'

Hoover was so blasé about the effects of the depression on ordinary people that shortly before the end of his term in 1932 he gave orders for General Douglas MacArthur to clear out demonstrators camping in shanty towns in Washington DC. MacArthur used bayonets and tear gas, and in the 'Battle of Anacostia Flats' an eleven-month-old baby died, allegedly from exposure to CS fumes.

It wasn't good electioneering. Three months later the American people gave him their verdict – a decisive thumbs down.

A more tragic own-goal was the 16mm film made in September 1963 by President John F. Kennedy and some of his friends depicting a mock assassination. Kennedy's own idea, it was shot on a jetty at the private estate of Hugh and Janet Auchinloss, and showed friends and aides, and finally Jackie Kennedy, stepping over his body.

According to Robert Knudsen, President Kennedy, who was shot dead in Dallas two months later, wrote the script and even provided a bag of red liquid to use as imitation 'blood'.

Though if ever there was a 'natural' Presidential own goal scorer it was Gerald Ford. The slow-speaking former football player, who boasted of being 'the first Eagle Scout President of the USA', had a real predilection for boners.

He told how, whenever he could, he 'always watched the Detroit Tigers on radio'. He said he was 'a moderate on domestic issues, a conservative in fiscal affairs, and a dyed-in-the-wool internationalist in foreign affairs.'

The man who was so nervous on his wedding day, he wore one brown shoe and one black shoe, bumbled and fumbled in 1974 when questioned by a group of businessmen in Palm Springs about South-East Asia:

'The situation in Cambodia is, uh, one of the most confused that we, or other nations, face in, uh, diplomacy or military circumstances. It's a very complex situation when you have, uh, the People's Republic of China, to a degree, anyhow, however, until recently, apparently, supporting Prince Sihanouk.

'The implications are, uh, hard to detect, at the moment. In the meantime, it's a difficult situation, uh, but for us to leave with those other forces all confused, uh, would be a mistake, in my judgment.'

Who did he say was confused?

President Ford's wit may have been slow but his judgment was sure. Jimmy Carter's mind was sharp but his judgment disastrous. The architect of the unfortunate mission to rescue the US hostages in Iran, who collapsed before TV cameras while out jogging, and who admitted to being almost savaged by a bunny rabbit, was fond of pronouncements such as this one, in February 1977: 'There is no single member of the Cabinet in whom I have any disappointment . . . Bert Lance is the key to the entire process of budgeting and reorganisation, and has been tremendous in his job.'

Two months later Mr Lance quit.

Mr Carter's uniquely blasé style of blundering into problems was summed up in a diary entry just three months before the American public gave him a very decisive thumbs down: 'I have got problems on my shoulders but, strangely enough, I feel better as they pile up. . . .'

But if there was one great own goal in the history of the Presidency, it had to be President Nixon's gradual and irreversible slide to disgrace in Watergate. In 1972, RN wasn't going to be satisfied unless he won every state, plus Washington DC. So his aides began a campaign of burglary, bugging and dirty tricks that was to land most of them in jail, exile, or oblivion.

Well, as Richard Nixon himself said to Elliot Richardson: 'You must pursue this investigation, even if it leads to the President.' And: 'The important thing is the presidency. If needs be, save the presidency from the president.'

After all, this was the man who said in 1966: 'The press are good guys. They are very helpful with their questions.'

And, according to aides of Nelson Rockefeller, leant back laughing behind his desk in the Oval Office and, amid much mirth, asked:

'Can you imagine Jerry Ford sitting in this chair!!?'

10 Top Gaffes by US Presidents

1 This is a great day for France.
Richard Nixon, in Paris for the
funeral of President Pompidou, 1974

2 That is a discredited president.
Richard Nixon, in a speech in 1974
during the Watergate scandal. He
meant 'precedent'

3 The United States has much to offer the third world war.
Ronald Reagan, in an address to third
world nations in 1975. He made the
same mistake nine times

4 To you, and to the people you represent, the great people of the government of Israel.
Gerald Ford toasting Anwar Sadat,
President of Egypt, at a dinner in
Washington DC 1975

5 When we get back, I think we ought to write him another letter – just cold and very blunt.
Jimmy Carter as an aside to Cy Vance
during talks with Indian premier
Morarji Desai, January 1978. The
microphones picked up – and
broadcast – every word

6 I desire the Poles carnally.
Jimmy Carter, mistranslated by
rookie aide, Warsaw, 1978

7 I've talked to you on a number of occasions about the economic problems our nation faces ... And I am prepared to tell you it's in a hell of a mess.
Ronald Reagan, rehearsal for White
House broadcast, November 1982.
He then asked: 'We're not connected
to the press room yet, are we?' They
were.

✓ 8   I would like to extend a warm welcome to Chairman Mo.
Ronald Reagan, on visit of President
Doe of Liberia to Washington, August
1982

9   I ask you to join me in a toast to President Figueiredo and the people of Bolivia. . . . No, that's where I'm going.
Ronald Reagan in Brazil, December
1982 (and D minus again – he really
was off to Bogotá, Colombia)

10   My fellow Americans. I am pleased to tell you I just signed legislation that will outlaw Russia forever. We begin bombing in five minutes.
Ronald Reagan, spoof announcement
to radio engineers shortly before his
weekly broadcast, August 1984. Its
subsequent airing hardly went down a
bomb with the public.

Election Own Goals

He dithered. He dallied. He teased the nation by appearing on television and singing an embarrassing little ditty about 'there was I, waiting at the church.' He told all his senior staff and friends he was calling an October election. Then changed his mind.

The procrastination in September 1978 undoubtedly cost Prime Minister James Callaghan his job. And it plunged the Labour party into an internal turmoil from which it had to struggle to recover.

In September 1982, when Mr Callaghan had the chance to go for an October election, the Tories' lead was just 2 per cent – down from 6 per cent in July.

By the end of October, when the poll might have been, Labour had built a solid lead of five-and-a-half points. They would have won handsomely.

In the event, the election was delayed until May and 'Sunny Jim' made another monster own goal, coming back tanned from a summit in Guadeloupe and scoffing about a strike of lorry drivers. Mrs Thatcher was swept into power as Labour suffered the heaviest defeat of an incumbent government since the war.

George Romney, Republican Governor of Michigan, was a strongish challenger for the 1968 nomination eventually won by Richard Nixon – until he scored a dramatic own goal. Granted a facility to visit US troops in Vietnam, he talked foolishly on his return about how he had 'just had the biggest brainwashing that anybody could get out there.' He was finished, withdrawing even before the first primary. To Governor James Rhodes of Ohio, watching him go after the nomination was 'like watching a duck trying to make love to a football'.

Another man they said was finished, wrongly as it turned out, was New York Governor Nelson Rockefeller. In 1966, about to try for a third term, he was seen as the villain of two tax hikes. There had been criticism about his appointees, there had been scandals over liquor and medicare. Friends told him: 'You can't win.'

A pundit said: 'He is politically dead. He is about as popular as measles.' His private pollster said: 'You couldn't be elected dog catcher.'

Well, they were all wrong. Rocky won.

The most complete barrage of election own goal scoring so far seen came from the Labour Party in the British general election of 1983. If ever a team threw it away they did.

POW! Labour Party General Secretary Jim Mortimer managed to discourage the party faithful by saying: 'We have a good way to go before we can win. We are not yet ready.'

CRACK! In a TV programme Labour heavy Denis Healey lost thousands of votes when he accused Mrs Thatcher of 'glorying in slaughter' over the Falklands.

ZAP! Welsh wonder boy Neil Kinnock went further than Mr Healey. He said Mrs Thatcher had guts 'but it's a pity people had to leave theirs at Goose Green to prove it.'

SLOSH! Denis Healey was red-faced again after a letter showed his doublethink on the Falklands. He told a constituent

British banks had 'no alternative but to throw good money after bad' in Argentina. A pity, since he'd been accusing Mrs Thatcher of 'stupefying hypocrisy' in supporting British loans to Argentina.

POWEE! Ex-Premier James Callaghan lambasted Labour policy on unilateral disarmament. At the Labour Party conference at Brighton in October, he was hissed and booed as he said: 'You made a fundamental mistake in believing that by going on marches and passing resolutions you could carry the votes of the British people. You lost millions of votes.' In keeping with the spirit of the Labour campaign others shouted back: 'No, you did.'

Perhaps the loneliest figure after the 1983 campaign was Labour Party leader Michael Foot, who led his party to a drubbing (all the time prophesying glorious victory), and was hastily replaced afterwards. His shambling performance at the Cenotaph in 1981 set the tone for a dismal leadership of his party. The 1983 Labour manifesto was described by Peter Shore as 'the longest suicide note in history' but Mr Foot blamed the media, the pollsters, the Tory government – anybody but himself. His book after 'retiring' *Another Heart and Other Pulses* was said by one critic to have had the most appropriate of working titles: *Own Goal.*

One candidate who openly courted disaster was Mr Graham Gopsill, Liberal candidate for Birmingham Hodge Hill at the June 1983 election. Mr Gopsill took off for a honeymoon in Brittany, pausing only to send a card to his constituents saying: 'Having a great time – don't forget to vote for me.'

His agent, John Aldridge, said: 'He hopes none of his supporters in Hodge Hill will feel he has deserted them. He is having a nice holiday and is looking forward to coming back to Birmingham on Saturday.'

Mr Gopsill was said to be 'confident of the result'. So confident, in fact, that he did not even want his night's sleep interrupted to be told what it was.

He polled 6557 votes – a massive 13 000 less than the winning Labour candidate.

But if Mr Gopsill was a cheery loser, he could hardly rival Commander William George Boaks with his one-man Democratic Monarchist Public Safety White Resident Party. Losing his deposit in 26 by-elections starting in Walthamstow in 1951, Mr Boaks finally got into the record books at the Glasgow Hillhead by-election in March 1982.

He scored five votes – the lowest attained by any candidate in the history of British universal suffrage.

In November 1982, at the age of 79, Mr Boaks had to retire – though not so much through lack of steam as through having lost his entire life savings of £4000 in forfeited deposits.

Mr Timothy Smith, counsel to President Carter in his downhill 1980 election campaign, had an astonishing tip-off: that Reagan aides had managed to get hold of secret campaign briefing papers and would be able to check Mr Carter's every move in the vital TV debate between the two candidates.

Mr Smith thought the idea 'implausible' and did not do anything about it.

Later, in what became dubbed 'Debategate', it was revealed Reagan aides *had* got the briefing papers . . . and were able to blunt Carter's otherwise guaranteed edge in the TV debate.

Mr Smith's holding of high political office is now also considered 'implausible'.

In the 1964 election, Conservative Party Chairman Lord Blakenham had a message for Liberal supporters: 'A Liberal vote is a wasted vote.' A good many Liberals took his advice. They voted Labour. Lord Blakenham's party were out of office after 13 years.

The British general election of 1970 caused a major upset. Everybody thought Harold Wilson and Labour were set to romp home.

On election night, June 18, champagne was readied at Transport House, London, as supporters gathered for the formal victory party. Across Smith Square at Conservative Central Office, party workers prepared for an early night.

Then something astonishing happened. In the BBC studios in Lime Grove, the 'swingometer' specially prepared for pundit

Robert Mackenzie and showing various Labour majorities had to be hurriedly repainted as the first seat, Guildford, showed a 6 per cent swing to Conservatives.

At Conservative HQ there was a frantic rush to find drinks for a celebration none had expected.

Mr Wilson was more surprised than most when he was shunted out of 10 Downing Street the following morning. With foolhardy self-confidence he had not even thought of preparing somewhere to live in case he lost.

But an even more astonishing election own goal was the exhausted Welsh returning officer who announced the wrong candidate as winner . . . with everyone else at the count too tired to notice. And yet his pronouncement was legally binding!

Mr Trevor Sayce-Davies, 70, had to go to the High Court in 1983 to reverse the result for the fifth seat to the community council at Grosmont, near Abergavenny. Despite winning, he found he could not be sworn in and his defeated opponent had taken his seat in the council chamber.

Mr Sayce-Davies and Mrs Rosamund Rocyn-Jones, a 44 year old housewife, had tied with 79 votes each after six recounts. Neither would agree to the tossing of a coin, but they agreed to pick two pieces of paper, one with a cross on, from a policeman's cap.

Said Mr Sayce-Davies: 'I said "ladies first" and Mrs Rocyn-Jones picked her paper. Then I went up to get mine. I picked the one with the cross.

'Mrs Rocyn-Jones came over and shook my hand and congratulated me and then my wife.'

Mr Sayce-Davies then went up the road for a coffee while his opponent went to collect her daughter from a babysitter. In the absence of both, the returning officer Mr George Cummings sleepily and irretrievably announced the wrong result.

In the High Court, Mr Justice Comyn asked Mr John Male, acting for Mr Sayce-Davies: 'Why was there not a hullabulloo at the time he announced the result?'

Well you know politics and politicians.

'I think people at the count were suffering from fatigue, m'lud,' replied Mr Male.

Finally, Dr Garret Fitzgerald seemed sure-footed enough as he campaigned to be the next Prime Minister of Ireland in 1982. But on a tour of Cavan and Monaghan, the sight of the leader of Fine Gael brought giggles from would-be voters.

He was wearing odd shoes. On his right foot, he displayed a black brogue, on his left, an equally black but smooth and shiny shoe.

Anguished aides explained he had a tough programme that day, and not wanting to wake his wife, he had dressed in the dark.

That's a politician for you – a foot in both camps.

Albatrosses – 20 Careless Phrases which Returned to Haunt World Leaders

1 Wait and see.

H. H. Asquith, British PM, 1910

2 What is our task? To make Britain a fit country for heroes to live in.

David Lloyd-George, British PM, 1918

3 Safety first.

Stanley Baldwin, British PM, campaign slogan, 1929

4 When more and more people are thrown out of work, unemployment results.

Calvin Coolidge, ex-US President, 1930

5 Peace in our time.

Neville Chamberlain, British PM, returning from Munich with the famous 'piece of paper' signed by Hitler, 1938

6   They've never had it so good.
Harold Macmillan, British PM,
speech at Bedford, 1957

7   I should be in favour of giving the Russians an ultimatum, and if necessary, conducting a total war.
Henry Kissinger, US academic, 1959

8   I could never be Prime Minister. I do my sums with matchsticks.
Lord Home interviewed by Kenneth
Harris, 1962

9   We are not going to send American boys nine or ten thousand miles to do what Asian boys ought to be doing for themselves.
Lyndon B. Johnson, US President,
1964

10   We are going to build a Great Society – where no man is the victim of fear or poverty or hatred, where every man has a chance for fulfilment, prosperity, and hope.
Lyndon B. Johnson, 1964

11   The permissive society has been allowed to become a dirty phrase. A better phrase is the civilized society.
Roy Jenkins, British Labour Home
Secretary, 1966

12   Devaluation does not mean, of course, that the pound here in Britain, in your pocket or purse, or in your bank has been devalued.
Harold Wilson, British PM,
devaluation broadcast, 1967

13   Polacks.
US Vice-President, Spiro Agnew, on
Polish-Americans, 1968

14 Most of us have stopped using silver every day.
Margaret Thatcher, British Education
Minister, 1970

15 If it takes a bloodbath, let's get it over with.
Ronald Reagan, Governor of
California, on police action against
student demonstrators, 1970

16 Let us pledge to make these four years the best four years in American history.
Richard Nixon, US President,
inaugural address, 1973

17 I don't believe the Poles consider themselves dominated by the Soviet Union.
Gerald R. Ford, US President, election
TV debate with Jimmy Carter, 1976

18 Other than when playing darts, I become confused at the mere mention of figures.
Neil Kinnock, House of Commons,
1978

19 Please don't run your country down by talking of mounting chaos. (Translated by *Sun* headline writers to 'Crisis – What Crisis?').
James Callaghan, British PM, arriving
suntanned and relaxed from
Guadeloupe summit during lorry
drivers' strike, 1979

20 Reaganomics are voodoo economics.
George Bush candidate for the
Republican presidential nomination,
1980

4

It Takes a Crook to Catch a Crook, or of Course Crime Doesn't Pay

Blow It!

It had all the makings of the perfect crime. No one saw the three raiders as they broke into the factory in Vang, central Norway, in August 1977. No one disturbed them as they located the company safe and primed a small explosive charge to blow off the door.

Calmly they set the fuse and retired to the safety of the next room. Then came a small explosion.

Well, a large explosion. . . .

It brought the factory crashing down around the hopeless threesome in a great roar of flying bricks, mortar and smoke.

Unfortunately for the crooks, the safe hadn't contained money. It had been full of dynamite.

Similarly explosive results followed the antics of a gang of blundering burglars in Sydney, Australia, in September 1983.

The first time they tried to blow the safe at the post office in a Sydney suburb, they didn't manage to open it up. They escaped with just 53 dollars.

So . . . they returned with more gelignite.

It was a bigger explosion this time. So big, it wrecked the post office building, blowing out all the windows and lifting the roof off the walls.

Worse still, the thieves had to leave empty-handed. The massive blast had jammed the door of the safe.

Bored bachelor Kevin Jones had what he thought was a bright idea for getting free groceries. The unemployed 25 year old went round supermarkets tearing the child's face off more than 300 tins of Heinz baby food. He was able to use them on special offer vouchers for free shopping.

Stourbridge magistrates heard in July 1983 how the label trek enabled Jones to claim £15 worth of free groceries from Asda stores. But as well as landing him a £100 fine, there was one other fault with his scheme. It had cost him £16 travelling round the Midlands to collect the labels.

A student from Bakersfield, California, appeared in court charged with stealing a record album. Its title: 'Thou shall not steal'.

In April 1984, Yeovil magistrates heard how two burglars had botched a raid on a grocery store. The 'cash box' they stole turned out to be . . . the burglar alarm.

James Landis, 29, nearly pulled off a sensational 'first' crime when he managed to sneak $128,000 out of the 'unrobbable' US Mint in an old paper bag. It was a massive sum in 1953.

He managed to substitute wads of blank paper for bundles of notes in the storeroom, and reckoned he had six months to make his getaway abroad before the bundles were sent out to banks and opened.

He overlooked one thing – the heavy printing on finished notes. His dummy packages were 21 ounces lighter than the real thing. When another loader noticed the weight difference, all police had to do was to look for the Mint man spending the most $20 notes.

Still on the big money, Constantine Econopoulos tried his hand at the giant slot machine at Harrah's casino in Lake Tahoe, Nevada, and hit the jackpot. It had been 19 months since the last payout and Mr Econopoulos netted a cool $1.1 million.

The inevitable news and publicity pictures followed, and Mr Econopoulos' champagne-splashed good fortune was shown across America on the early evening news in September, 1983.

But police in San Francisco were more interested than most in seeing the winner's happy smiling face. To them he was 'Gus the runt', a well known petty criminal.

In the chase by Lake Tahoe agents that followed, 'Gus the runt' was tracked to Texas where he admitted he had collected the money after others had rigged the one-armed bandit's delicate silicon-chip electronics.

If he'd only asked for no publicity. . . .

Many crooks fail because they try to take on too much. In a word, greed.

A Chicago preacher suffered 29 car crashes, two burglaries, a touch of food poisoning and 21 falls, all within two years.

It was the 30th car crash that did it. The insurance company refused to believe him. They compared notes with other insurers and found every claim had been fraudulent.

He should have tried another dose of food poisoning.

Others underestimate the resistance of the public. A hijacker on a Northwest Airlines flight from Tampa to Miami in 1983 held a knife to a stewardess's throat and ordered: 'Take me to Cuba.'

He needed hospital treatment after being attacked, beaten, and finally bound by six angry passengers. Among the indignities he suffered were a dousing in the washroom, being suspended upside down, kicked, punched, being tied up with seat belts and finally having two of the heftiest passengers sit on him.

It's comforting to know that felons can end up looking as foolish as the rest of us. A mugger who 'hit' Roger Morse of Winnipeg, Canada, in December 1983, messed it up after he had emptied his victim's wallet of $30 – he handed back his own wallet by mistake. While the thief made a swift getaway from the scene, Roger was left counting a surprise windfall of $300.

Two bank robbers became the most photographed raiders in American history when they blundered from a bank job . . . straight into a mammoth publicity stunt.

Five thousand people had gathered outside the Empire State Building in March 1982, waiting for thousands of dollars to be thrown from the roof to promote an adult education course.

With towering incompetence, the raiders ran straight from

the bank they had just robbed into the melee – and became tangled in TV cables. One hundred citizens joined in their arrest – to the delight of the waiting cameramen.

The pilot of a light plane carrying £200 000 worth of drugs to Britain from Morocco was rumbled when he blundered right into the middle of a NATO exercise, Gloucester Crown Court heard in June 1984.

The ultimate in high-flying dramas came after the single-engined Piper Cherokee suddenly found itself flying alongside an RAF Phantom jet, bristling with Sidewinder missiles. The intruder's plane number was radioed to base, and the pilot was arrested as he came in to land at Bristol airport.

Still in the air: on a flight across the United States, a would-be hijacker pulled a gun, pointed it at a stewardess, and demanded: 'Take me to Detroit.'

'That's where we're meant to be going,' she said.

'Oh good,' said the gunman, and promptly sat down again.

Some crooks come unstuck a little later, in that theatre of villainy, the courtroom.

Like the defendant who rather gave the game away when appearing at Croydon magistrates' court in December 1963. When asked by Mr John Clay, prosecuting 'Are you making up your evidence as you go along,' the accused replied: 'Do you think I could make up all these lies?'

Spare a thought for the jewel thief who, at Preston Crown Court in November 1983, was about to plead not guilty to a case involving stolen gems . . . when his wife walked into court wearing some of the loot. One of the victims immediately recognised the distinctive diamond and sapphire ring she sported.

Mr Peter Openshaw, prosecuting, said her appalling foolishness had given her husband's planned defence 'something of a hollow ring.' He changed his plea to guilty.

A Noose for their Necks – 10 Notorious Murderers and how they Gave the Game Away

1 TRAPPED BY A GALLSTONE

'You can't prove murder without a body,' small-time con man John George Haigh taunted police when quizzed about the disappearance of rich widow Mrs Olive Durand-Deacon. They proved him very wrong. Confident of his success, Haigh boasted: 'I have destroyed her with acid. You will find the sludge which remains in Leopold Road. Every trace of her has gone.'

But in the sludge, famed pathologist Professor Keith Simpson found first, a gallstone, and then, Mrs Durand-Deacon's acrylic dentures. Haigh was trapped. He subsequently admitted eight other murders, his plea of insanity was rejected, and he was hanged at Wandsworth jail, London, on 10 August 1949.

If he had chosen nitric instead of sulphuric acid – indeed, if he had waited three more weeks by which time all trace of the wealthy widow *would* have gone – Haigh would not have been brought to trial. His senseless bragging to police literally made a noose for his neck.

2 HE WENT ON OFFERING POISONED SCONES

Major Herbert Rowse Armstrong was a small town solicitor in Hay-on-Wye, Herefordshire. In February 1921, he successfully disposed of his nagging wife, Katherine, with a huge dose of arsenic, managing to persuade the local doctor she had died from natural causes and to record 'gastritis' on the death certificate.

Flushed with his success, the major then kept inviting his rival lawyer across the street, Mr Oswald Martin, to tea and scones. Mr Martin was suspicious of this sudden bonhomie, all the more so when after one tea party he became violently ill. He called the police. As a result of their investigation, Mrs Armstrong was exhumed. Her body was full of poison. Armstrong, the man who refused to quit while ahead, went to the gallows in 1922.

3 HE CARRIED ON CONFESSING

RAF deserter Frederick Field managed to get a large sum from the *News of the World* by confessing to a murder he didn't commit and, at the trial, withdrawing his confession at the last minute. So pleased was he, he tried the same technique again. Unfortunately for him the second time the jury believed his retracted confession and he was hanged.

Field's first confession was that he had killed Norah Upchurch, a 31-year-old prostitute whose strangled body was found by workmen in October 1931, in an empty building in Shaftesbury Avenue. He could not possibly have committed the crime as his description of it did not all tie in with the facts. But he obtained a large sum from the newspaper, who agreed to pay his defence costs if acquitted.

In 1936 Field was arrested as a deserter and, no doubt trying to improve his fortunes once again, immediately confessed to the murder of Beatrice Vilna Sutton, a middle-aged widow found suffocated to death in her flat. Field's story was much better this time. So good, in fact, that when he tried to withdraw it at the last minute the jury chose to believe the original confession. He was hanged in June 1936.

4   LEFT HIS SPECS AT THE SCENE

Nathan Leopold, 19, was the son of one of Chicago's wealthiest and most prominent families. It was one of America's most sensational murder trials when, in 1924, he appeared with the son of the Vice-President of Sears-Roebuck, 18-year-old Richard Loeb, charged with the murder of 14-year-old Bobby Franks.

Leopold had scored two major 'own goals'. First a pair of spectacles was found at the scene, and when questioned Leopold said: 'If I were not positive that my glasses were at home, I would say these are mine.' But he could not produce them.

Second, a ransom note for $10 000 matched exactly the print from Leopold's typewriter. His alibi was in tatters.

It was later revealed the two boys had decided 'for kicks' to try and commit the perfect crime. It didn't work out that way. Both were imprisoned for life, Leopold being freed in 1958, and dying in 1971. Loeb was killed in a prison homosexual brawl in 1936, launching the immortal newspaper headline: 'Sentence ends with a proposition.'

5   SHE TALKED TOO MUCH

Ethel Lillie Major was a 43-year-old gamekeeper's daughter who literally talked her way to the gallows. When her husband Arthur died in severe pain in May 1934, a doctor certified the cause of death as 'status epilepticus'. Police received an anonymous letter claiming Mr Major had taken a mistress and as a result, been poisoned by his wife. They didn't take it too seriously at first. But when they went to interview her she astonished them by saying: 'I didn't know my husband had died of strychnine poisoning.'

Told that no one had even mentioned strychnine, Mrs Major said: 'Oh, I'm sorry, I must have made a mistake.' She certainly had. She was found guilty and executed in Hull jail in December 1934.

6   HE COULDN'T SPELL HAMPSTEAD

Horace William 'Bertie' Manton, a driver in the fire service, was trapped as the notorious 'Luton Sack Murderer' because he left the 'p' out of a simple London place name.

In November 1943, the strangled body of a woman was found in a sack in the River Lea near Luton. Her face had been mutilated to try to prevent her being identified. But her coat was found, and in it, a dry-cleaning tag. This was traced to a Luton shop and a Mrs Caroline Manton.

Bertie Manton denied the woman in the sack was his wife, and to 'prove' it he produced a bundle of letters allegedly written to him by his absent spouse. Detectives noticed how 'Mrs Manton' kept talking not of Hampstead but of 'Hamstead'. They then asked Manton to jot down a few notes for them . . . including the tell-tale place name. Sure enough, he spelled it 'Hamstead'.

Manston was ordered to hang but his sentence was commuted to life imprisonment. He served three years before dying in prison in 1947.

7   HE PICKED UP THE WRONG HAT

Franz Muller, a 25-year-old German tailor, was convicted of Britain's first train murder after he picked up the wrong headpiece by mistake.

In July 1864, Thomas Briggs, aged 70, chief clerk of a London bank, was found dead on the railway line between Hackney Wick and Bow. It was quickly established he had been attacked in a first class compartment and in the compartment was found a cut-down topper identified as belonging to one Franz Muller.

In his haste after the murder, Muller had taken the wrong hat.

Muller had fled to America on the SS *Victoria* but police were there at New York to meet him . . . they had simply taken a faster liner.

Hanged in November 1864, before a large crowd, the case was such a *cause célèbre* the Muller hat even became fashion for a time.

8   SHE REFUSED TO DIET

Famous Canadian murderess Marguerite Pitre might have escaped detection if she had only cut down on the calories. In September 1949, 23 people died when a Quebec Airways DC3 on a flight from Montreal to Seven Islands exploded in mid-air over Cap Tourmente.

There was a sensation when it was revealed the cause of the explosion was a bomb in the aircraft's forward baggage compartment.

As a murder hunt began, everybody remembered the 'fat middle-aged woman' who had caused a stir when arriving with a parcel to be put aboard the plane at the very last minute. She had arrived in a taxi and made no attempt to disguise herself.

It was soon discovered that the husband of one of the plane's passengers, M. Albert Guay, had as his mistress a 'fat, middle-aged woman'. She was soon identified as Marguerite Pitre. Guay, Pitre and her brother were all hanged in 1951 for the murder of Mrs Guay and 22 other passengers and crew.

9   TRAPPED BY A 1500-YEAR-OLD SKULL

When, in 1983, homosexual Peter Reyn-Bart of Knightsbridge was questioned by police over an allegation he had butchered his waitress bride-of-convenience, Malika, 23 years before, he emphatically denied it. He said she had left him in 1962 to go and work in the Middle East.

But then police dug up a skull in a peat bog near his former home at Wilmslow, Cheshire. Confronted with news of this find, Reyn-Bart confessed to strangling his wife, chopping her body up with an axe and burying or burning her remains. He was jailed for life at Manchester Crown Court.

Reyn-Bart had talked himself into unnecessary trouble. When sent away for forensic examination, the skull was found to date to 410 AD – before the Roman legions left Britain. Until his confession, the police had no evidence against him.

10   HE BLABBED TO THE PRESS

In 1924, a rather unsuccessful young chicken farmer called Norman Thorne was interviewed by *Daily Express* crime reporter Percy Hoskins about the mysterious disappearance of his fiancée, Miss Elsie Cameron. Hoskins asked him if he was bothered by the continued police presence. 'I don't mind what they do as long as they don't disturb my chickens,' replied Thorne.

The police were getting nowhere and one senior detective asked Hoskins what he thought of the case. 'You'll find Elsie Cameron under the chicken run,' he said. They did, under several inches of earth. Thorne was hanged at Wandsworth in April 1925.

It's a Stick-up

Eddie Blake sauntered up to the bank cashier in Reno, Nevada, in 1983, and handed her a note: 'This is a hold-up – put all the money into a bag and hand it over.'

Within minutes he was making good his escape through the city streets, together with his loot.

But police were waiting for empty-headed Eddie when he got back home. He'd scrawled his note on an envelope. On the back were his name and address.

In November 1978 another bank robber threatened to blow up a branch of Barclays Bank in Middlesex if the manager did not leave £15 000 in cash in a bag outside an AA call box on the Staines bypass.

But he was foiled when his letter, posted first class, arrived twelve hours after the bomb was supposed to have gone off.

Another raider at a branch of Lloyds Bank in Verwood, Dorset, in February 1980 pushed an elderly woman customer aside as he swaggered to the counter.

But the cashier told him: 'I'm not having that. Go to the end of the queue.'

'This is a raid,' said the armed, masked bandit, slamming a duffel bag on to the counter for his plunder.

The cashier stood his ground. 'I don't care,' he said. 'You'll have to wait your turn.'

'Oh, Christ,' muttered the raider – and fled.

It's a tough world for the armed robber – anything can happen and frequently does.

New York is the bank-raid capital.

Among recent own goals: the tearaway who successfully robbed a bank, but then was caught when he tried to open an account at a branch nearby.

There was another robber who stormed into a bank, only to find another raid in progress. He apologised and left.

A third made his getaway through the city streets on a bicycle. Unfortunately he couldn't pedal very fast. He was caught by a policeman chasing him on foot.

Two crooks in Britain's West Midlands attempted seven sawn-off shotgun raids in one day in 1983 . . . and goofed them all.

RAID No. 1 came at a jewellery shop in Walsall. The younger accomplice recognised one of the assistants. They left.

RAID No. 2 . . . another Walsall jeweller's. They were scared off by the security cameras.

RAID Nos 3 and 4: A post office and supermarket at Cannock, Staffs. Aborted because 'too many people about'.

RAID No. 5 . . . A supermarket at Pelsall. Unfortunately when the raiders arrived it had just closed.

RAID No. 6: A private house in Yoxall. The householder wouldn't let them in.

RAID No. 7: Another private house. The man of the house woke up and chased them off with a walking stick.

It was no laughing matter though, when the antics of the bungling twosome landed them at Stafford Crown Court. The leader of the 'gang' was sentenced to six years' jail. His 17-year-old 'oppo' was given three years' youth custody.

Gerald MacDonnell gave himself a bit of Dutch courage to rob a building society. Unfortunately, a bit too much Dutch courage.

For as he lurched into the Provincial Building Society's branch in Edgware, Middlesex, he didn't realise . . . he had forgotten to disguise himself.

The £643 he escaped with was hardly a consolation next day when he saw his face staring out of the nation's newspapers . . . he had been photographed during the raid by security cameras.

Pleading guilty to the raid at the Old Bailey in January 1984, MacDonnell told how he had behaved like a foolish amateur, 'not bothering to spend a few pence on a stocking mask'.

The man who got tight rather than tights was jailed for three years.

Another bungling raider chose the wrong day when he tried to hold up a newspaper office in May 1979.

For the journalists were on strike, the newspaper was being given away free and there was no money on the premises.

To make it worse, when he appeared at the *Belfast Telegraph* brandishing a toy gun, one of the employees chased him away with a brush.

In Paris, an armed robber scooped up £4000 in cash, stuffed it into his bag, zipped it up, and walked slowly backwards towards the door, ordering everyone to keep still.

Nobody did. In fact, several of them leapt on him and held him down until police arrived. The unfortunate robber hadn't just zipped up the money. He had zipped up his pistol in the bag as well.

Raider Clive Castro leaped into the waiting car outside a city bank in Cooperville, Texas, and shouted 'Drive off quick before the cops get here.'

But the getaway driver had already got the message. In fact, he'd got away.

Castro was sitting in a *patrol* car, which took him straight to the nearest police station.

A madcap robber phoned a bank in Hollywood in the summer of 1983 and said: 'Leave $100 000 at the restaurant opposite, or I will explode a remote control bomb I have hidden in your vault.'

The petrified manager told him: 'But there isn't a restaurant opposite.'

'Oh, sorry,' came the reply. 'Wrong number.'

Finally, an even zanier robber appeared at a drive-in bank at Del Ray Beach, Florida, in October 1980, apparently having modelled himself on a character out of a Peter Sellers film.

Cooly he handed the note over to the cashier as he kept a parcel he was holding clearly in view.

'I got a bum,' the note read. 'I can blow you sky height. This is a held up.'

The cashier passed it to another clerk . . . and another. They all fell about laughing.

Angry and emptyhanded the raider sped off into the night.

Taking his 'bum' with him.

Stop Thief!

A valet wanted in connection with a big jewel robbery in Switzerland made a bad choice of hiding places. He tried to 'disappear' in Madrid during Interpol week. He was spotted by a visiting detective and promptly arrested.

Two gunmen who tried to rob a railway booking office, also in Switzerland, left no fingerprints at the scene. But they forgot it was snowing at the time. Police simply followed their footprints, straight to their homes.

Some thieves, well they simply ask to be arrested.

An Irishman who broke into a branch of the Midland Bank in Newcastle-upon-Tyne in 1983, fell asleep . . . and locked himself in.

Dozy Paul Kiernan, 22, from Dublin, got a three-month jail sentence in January 1984, after telling how he had trapped himself in the bank with a haul of just £2.64.

'Believe it or not, my client had some money on deposit at the

Midland Bank and he had a considerable amount of money on him at the time,' said a bemused Mr Alan Williams, defending Kiernan.

'No one who isn't round the bend, or very drunk, would break into a police station,' said Mr Wilfred Alsager, defending two clients in Stockport, Cheshire, in June 1983. Unfortunately his clients, two youths, had done just that. They had shinned up a drainpipe and broken into the 'nick' at Cheadle, Greater Manchester, forcing their way into a cigarette machine with a truncheon.

They were each sentenced to six months' youth custody. It was, as they say, a fair cop.

Giovanni Nardi thought he had made a clean getaway after fleeing fraud charges in Genoa and escaping to South America. He was sentenced to 3½ years jail in his absence.

In March 1970, after eleven years, Nardi decided the heat was off and it was time to return to Italy.

Hailing a taxi, he asked to be driven to Martecantini, 200 miles away. But the driver didn't know the way and stopped to ask a passer-by for directions.

The passer-by was Bruno Ventori – the policeman who had hunted Nardi eleven years before.

Said the jubilant detective: 'It was a chance in a million.' Nardi began his delayed sentence shortly afterwards.

While stretching his legs at a border customs post near Como, Italy, in 1983, Luigi Giacomo noticed a customs man having trouble trying to get a cigarette going.

Helpful Luigi stepped forward with a brand new lighter and happily gave him a light.

It cost him a jail sentence and the profit of 30 000 Swiss-made lighters he was trying to smuggle through in his car. Another customs man was suspicious and ordered a search which revealed the hidden contraband.

The thief who robbed a supermarket in the Bronx in October 1977 left a rather obvious clue behind . . . his wooden leg. The makeshift limb came off when Richard Lennon, 27, fled hot-foot with a second gunman to their getaway car. With a little difficulty, and hopping on one leg, Lennon made it to the waiting Cadillac.

But armed with the artificial appendage, complete with white sock and black suede shoe, detectives had no trouble in tracing their man. After his mistake, they explained, his defence hadn't a leg to stand on.

Police called to the scene of a housebreaking in New York in 1983 thought the thief had made a clean getaway. Unfortunately for him, he had left one rather large clue behind . . . his dog.

At one policewoman's suggestion, they released the mutt to see if it would lead them to their man. Half a mile from the scene of the crime, the dog stopped at a door and barked to be let in.

The occupant could scarcely believe his eyes as the police were there with his unfaithful friend to arrest him. The hounded housebreaker was later jailed for two months.

Accused of mugging an elderly woman in 1983, a Newcastle-upon-Tyne youth had the perfect alibi . . . he was busy carrying out armed robbery at the time.

It turned out there was no evidence to link him with the mugging, and if he'd said nothing, he would have been freed.

But his frank confession to the armed heist at a filling station landed him 18 months' youth custody. Police said he was so keen to prove he was 'no animal,' and would not attack old ladies, that he gladly admitted to the more 'macho' crime.

A hungry thief in Badajoz, Spain, had an unusual plan for stealing some food.

Javiar Ortiz, 25, dressed as a nun and smuggled himself into the local convent in July 1984.

Two things gave him away. First, the leg of ham he hid under his habit made him look like the order's first pregnant sister.

Second, he should have realised that even Spanish nuns don't wear size ten wellington boots.

He was spotted by the Mother Superior, bundled into a storeroom by the other sisters and turned over to the police.

Three men whose car was being chased by police in May 1983, decided to dump their vehicle and flee across open country.

They stopped the car, split up, and ran off. But they could have chosen a better place to make their escape.

All three had run straight into the grounds of Hindip Hall, Worcester . . . headquarters of the West Mercia Police.

Three burglars who raided a house in Baytown, Texas, in January 1984, quite definitely talked too much.

After they had left with their booty, a parrot in the house was able to repeat their names to detectives.

Finally, there was a cheeky Colombian bandit Angelo Rodrigues, 23. He had perfected the art of 'snatch and run'.

His trick was to hang around the athletics stadium in Cali, Colombia, and when a car or coach was slowed down by traffic, he would snatch whatever he could through the vehicle's open window.

He always got away because of his knowledge of the back alleys, and his ability to run.

He saw rich pickings in the coach arriving for the Pan American Games in August 1971, and sure enough he was able to snatch a tracksuit, a travel bag, and two cameras.

He saw the coach was full of women. He knew that all the women would do was scream, so he ambled off.

But soon he realised the women weren't screaming. They were chasing after him.

Easily they overtook him, and an angry bevy of women dashed him to the ground and took their revenge.

His shirt torn, his hands bleeding, Angelo was turned over to the police.

This hadn't been any coachload of tourists. It had been the women's 100 metres finalists on their way back to the athletes' village.

5

Even Those Who Make the Rules Sometimes Can't Avoid Looking Fools . . .

Boomerangs for the Boys in Blue

Police stood guard for more than an hour over a 'safe' reported dumped by the side of the road at Halesowen, West Midlands in May 1983. Then they called in the heavy mob to move it.

Well, you know about safes. They're weighty things. A squad of hefty policemen pushed. A Land Rover with a winch and heavy towing gear pulled.

After much pulling and shoving the penny dropped. It wasn't a safe at all . . . police had been trying to 'arrest' an electricity junction box newly installed by the side of the road.

They hadn't been able to move it because it was cemented to the ground.

In January 1977, the policemen in the tiny Australian town of St Arnaud got a brand new £160 000 police station.

They were delighted.

It had offices, accommodation for 27 constables, showers for policewomen, and a 50-car parking area.

The trouble was, there were only three police at St Arnaud, all of them men. The station had been designed for the bustling Melbourne suburb of St Albans, 170 miles away. A clerk had made a mistake.

One of the daftest police own goals came after a double murder at Teddington, Middlesex, in 1953. Two teenage girls were hacked to death on the towpath, and detectives were frantic to find the murder weapon. The order went out: 'Find the axe!' Scores of police mounted an intensive search.

Meanwhile at a terraced house nearby, a man was chopping firewood. He was a police constable – and the axe he was using was the murder weapon.

He later explained he had found it in the back of a police car, and it had just seemed right for his duties around the house.

In June 1984, two policemen were wounded when two groups of under-cover officers mistook each other for terrorists and opened fire in Vittoria, Spain.

But the most deadly cops-and-cops shoot-out came in northern Italy in February 1967, after a woman phoned with a tip-off about a gang of armed smugglers.

Told the smugglers would arrive by night at a remote cottage to pick up arms and ammunition, a large force of armed plain-clothes men lay in wait nearby.

Suddenly, shadowy figures loomed out of the thick fog.

'Halt!' shouted one policeman. 'Halt!' came back the reply.

Shots were fired, and then a fierce gun battle raged which killed one man and wounded two others. But none was a smuggler.

Unfortunately, the woman tipster had phoned *two* police stations. Each had sent squads of marksmen without telling the other.

The man who died commanded the unit from Cremona. The two injured men came from the police post in nearby Codogno.

An alert New York City policeman spotted a suspicious, obviously criminal-looking type racing through the streets of Greenwich Village. He acted swiftly. A blow from his nightstick checked the suspect's progress.

Then the officer was surprised to be surrounded by an angry, gesticulating crowd.

The 'criminal type' had been actor James Coburn.

The angry bystanders were a Hollywood film crew. The alert cop had ruined one of the key scenes in the latest Coburn movie.

The police chief who put rookie policewoman Madeline Fletcher and old hand Walter Kalberer together in a patrol car in December 1975 must have wished he'd never bothered.

He ended the day minus two officers . . . for *both* ended up in hospital with gunshot wounds after rowing about who should drive.

The two argued as soon as they were on their way out to the car.

Round one went to 20-year-old Miss Fletcher. She sat behind the wheel and managed to fend off her colleague's attempts to move her.

Round two went to 34-year-old Kalberer. He called in the Flint, Michigan, police supervisor.

Then things hotted up.

Miss Fletcher got out of the car, went up to her partner and swung her night stick at him. He got out his night stick and fended her off.

She started to walk away . . . but then pulled her gun, and fired three times, shooting Kalberer in the leg. He replied with four shots. Two officers nearby also fired at her. She was hit in the chest.

Both were rushed to hospital for emergency surgery.

An amazing scene took place at 3 a.m. outside a jewellery store in Melbourne, Australia, in February 1980. The shop's owner had just caught an armed burglar trying to escape through an open window. Brandishing a rifle, he told the thief: 'Come out, or I'll shoot.' When the burglar threatened to shoot him instead, the owner fired a round into the shop.

Meanwhile, there arrived on the scene two men . . . both only dressed in socks and trousers and one chasing the other. It turned out they were a husband and another man he had just discovered in bed with his wife. They had fought . . . but the lover came off worst. He was now pursuing the husband.

The husband not looking where he was going, crashed into the shopkeeper. The shopkeeper thought he was the burglar's accomplice, and shot at him. He missed. The husband fainted.

The lover, however much he wanted to punch the husband, didn't think a stranger should try to mow him down just like that. So he laid into the shopkeeper.

It was up to the police to sort everything out, of course. Not too difficult. When they arrived the lover and the shopkeeper were still fighting, with the husband sprawled on the pavement. All three were arrested, then when one was found to be the shop owner, just the husband and the lover were charged with attempted robbery.

The burglar? He made a clean getaway over the rooftops.

One of the wackiest police own goals concerned the breath test machine at Smethwick police station, West Midlands. It got drunk.

When the fume counter started churning out readings that suggested drivers had twice as much alcohol in their bodies than blood, tests were made.

It was found that the machine had become befuddled by drink and had to be sent away to force headquarters to be 'dried out'.

Still in the West Midlands, after 26 years service, Coventry policeman Owen Thomas became a crime statistic in 1983 on his very last day with the force.

His car was 'nicked' from outside the police station.

At a siege in Oakland, California, police spent two hours telling a gunman through loud hailers to give himself up. They stopped when one of them realised he was standing right next to them . . . shouting to the non-existent occupant: 'Why don't you give yourself up?'

Forces Favourites

'Soldiers,' Napoleon told his troops as they prepared to fight the English at Waterloo: 'You are going to undertake a conquest of which effects on civilisation, and the commerce of the world, are incalculable. . . . You will give to England the most certain . . . death stroke. . . . We shall succeed in our enterprises. The fates are with us.'

Adolf Hitler was just as confident: 'I go with the assurance of a sleepwalker,' he said, 'on the path that providence dictates.'

'My God! This can't be true,' said US Secretary of the Navy Frank Knox in December 1941, when told that Japanese planes had attacked Pearl Harbour. 'They must mean the Philippines.'

Nowhere is the potential greater for the telling, lasting own goal than in the military.

We are not interested in the possibilities of defeat. They do not exist.
Queen Victoria, 1900, on the Boer War. Britain lost almost every battle

Who is this damned naval man who says we will want 3000 tanks? He talks like Napoleon.
British First World War General turning down the tank and staying with horses, 1916

The situation is splendid. God willing, we are going forward to great and victorious days.
Kaiser Wilhelm II, June 1918

The whole nation loves him, because it feels safe in his hands like a child in the arms of his mother.
Dr Joseph Goebbels on Adolf Hitler, 1934

This is a dull war. There is no shooting.
Prince Philip, 1940, when midshipman on HMS Valiant

If the British attack our cities we will simply erase theirs. The hour will come when one of us will break up, and it won't be Nazi Germany.
Adolf Hitler, September 1940

We are planning for the war against Japan to last until 1949. I expect to see our people in Tokyo before this thing is over though, unless we want war with another generation.
Admiral Frederick Horne, vice chief of US Naval Operations, July 1943

You never win a war without escalation.
Senator Barry Goldwater on Vietnam
April 1967

The role of the marines that went into Vietnam – I mean
Lebanon, a Freudian slip – one year ago has not changed.
General Paul X. Kelley, US Marine
Commandant, in Beirut, October
1983

Military Own Goals

It was like a silent comedy script from the golden days of
Hollywood. But it happened, all right. The pride of the US
Navy, the $50 million brand-new nuclear sub *Guitarro* sank to
the bottom of San Pablo Bay in 1969 while she was being fitted
out.

How? Well, it was the story of two crews. Working at each
end of the ship they managed to fill and empty the sub of water
without knowing the other was at work.

Up forward a non-nuclear crew pumped 3000 tons of water
into ballast tanks, to lower the bow and trim the ship for tests by
a nuclear crew down aft. They then trundled off for supper.

Astern the nuclear gang had decided the sub was already trim
and were simultaneously emptying five tons of water from *their*
tanks.

As the astonished forward crew came back from supper, there
was the *Guitarro*, down by the bow in 35 feet of water.

A Congressional committee called the sinking which resulted
in millions of dollars worth of damage, 'inexcusable careless-
ness'. But they refused to let the shipyard commander, Rear
Admiral Norbert Frankenberger, take all the blame, saying:
'The proximate causes of the catastrophe were the deficient
performance of the civilian supervisory personnel through
whom the shipyard commander must carry out his function,
and the duplicating, overlapping, and frequently conflicting
channels of command responsibility within the overall system.'

So now you know.

Still, that's the military. In August 1979, a Spanish air force jet managed to shoot itself down when its cannon fire richocheted off a hillside practice target. The pilot ejected to safety.

In August 1983, a Swedish minelayer on exercise managed to score a direct hit on itself with anti-aircraft barrage. The bridge of the 300 ft *Alvsborg* was badly damaged.

And off New South Wales in April 1977, the Australian destroyer-escort *Swan* managed to score a direct hit on the submarine, *Oxley*, having mistaken it for a practice target. An Australian naval spokesman said: 'Well, at least we hit what we were aiming for.'

Mind you, it's worth remembering that even Admiral Horatio Nelson was seasick at the Battle of Trafalgar.

Perhaps that was what happened among those commanding the Leander-class frigate *Jupiter* in June 1984, when the 2900 ton vessel tried a U-turn during a goodwill trip up the Thames and slammed beam-on into London Bridge causing £25 000 worth of damage. Forty sailors standing to attention on deck had to scurry for safety moments before the impact. 'They looked a right load of Wallies,' said an eye-witness, Mr Richard Friend.

A granite section of the bridge was dislodged but the frigate, which had just had a £68 million refit, fared worse, cancelling the rest of her visit and limping ignominiously back to base.

At a subsequent court martial her Captain, Commander Colin Hamilton, received a severe reprimand after being found guilty of negligence.

It had obviously not been his day, for after ordering the two tugs to pull the *Jupiter* off the parapet the inevitable happened. The frigate crunched into London Bridge a second time.

Four new minesweepers, the best that money could buy, were built for the Italian Navy at a shipyard in the River Magra, a mile from the Mediterranean, in September 1983.

Manufacturers Intermarine had equipped them with the most sophisticated modern technology. They were constructed of glass fibre to prevent the accidental adhesion of mines to their hulls.

There was just one problem. They were too big to pass under a bridge at the head of the river and into the sea.

Going back in time, perhaps the most costly naval own goal was in 1893 when Admiral Tryon tried to play dodgems with two columns of British battleships (just imagine, there's only one battleship in the whole western world right now, the USS *New Jersey*). From his flagship, Tryon reckoned it might look pretty to about-face the columns, reversing course by turning inwards. There wasn't room, of course, and the HMS *Camperdown* rammed HMS *Victoria*, which sank with many lives lost.

All Tryon's subordinate officers knew what was about to happen. Battleships are, after all, very big. But no one dared disobey the Admiral's orders.

Conveniently for the British, French, Americans and Canadians, Hitler took a sleeping pill as thousands of troops stormed the Normandy beaches on D-day. His aides were loath to upset him by waking him, which was all to the good since German forces were virtually paralysed without the orders of their commander-in-chief. The Fuhrer's slumbers helped win the day for the Allies.

Meanwhile the Germans were so convinced that Calais was going to be the starting point of the invasion, they treated the Normandy landings for some time as purely a diversionary attack. It was 42 days before German military intelligence conceded yes, this was the real thing.

The Italian armed forces came a cropper after an investigation by the country's Court of Accounts in 1971. There were some embarrassing revelations about the top brass in an important part of the NATO defences.

It was revealed Italy had 1063 generals – one for every 180 fighting men. Worse still, there were two Admirals for every warship.

Said Dr Baiamonti, a member of the Court of Accounts: 'It's worse then Fred Karno's army.'

In July 1984, more than 100 Spanish paratroopers celebrated an accident-free 'drop' with a five-star meal.

They were all rushed to hospital with food poisoning.

American columnist Jack Anderson told in August 1983 that two young missile launch officers in Kansas nearly sent a Titan intercontinental missile on its way to Russia.

When the missile men turned the keys to begin a test, controls signalled that the missile was about to launch. Luckily, they decided to turn the whole thing off. It turned out a maintenance crew had mixed up the wires differentiating between a test and an actual launch.

So we're all still here . . .

An embarrassing own goal for British military history was scored in 1982 when it was revealed senior officers had lost the Falklands surrender document signed by the Argentines.

Frantic searches went on for weeks among forces units throughout the country.

Finally, after three months, the surrender, signed on 14 June 1982, by General Menendez, Argentine commander in Port Stanley, turned up during a search of two boxes of Falklands papers at Royal Marines headquarters, Plymouth.

A Defence Ministry spokesman said: 'The documents weren't lost. They were mislaid.'

They don't call them the silent service for nothing. In 1972 the Royal Navy loaned the submarine HMS *Andrew* to the Welfare State Theatre Group who were putting on a show on the beach at Penzance, Cornwall.

The hero had to board the sub in search of a mermaid while actors carrying torches gathered round.

But the navy hadn't told anyone.

Besieged by calls from anxious residents who decided the sub had run aground and was sending out distress signals, coast-guards launched a full scale emergency rescue operation, even calling out the Penzance lifeboat.

Finally, let us spare a thought for the classic accompaniment to military might, the panoply of band and bugle.

General de Gaulle fumed for months over the French Armistice Day ceremony in 1963 which ended flatly on the wrong note: nobody cued the band to play *Le Marseillaise*.

In 1983, President Reagan hired the US Air Force's Singing

Sergeants to perform at a dinner in honour of Israeli Premier Yitzhak Shamir.

Their choice of programme was rather undiplomatic. Highlight of their performance was a rendering of their hit 'Soon I'll be done with the troubles of the world, I want to meet my Jesus.'

10 Five-Star Own Goals in Battle

1 CULLODEN, 1746

It was something rather different at Bannockburn, of course, but Culloden was complete disaster for the Scots under young pretender 'Bonnie' Prince Charles Edward Stuart. Starving and ill-equipped, 5000 of the Prince's bedraggled army took on some 9000 English redcoats. The battle lasted just 40 minutes. The Scots had no answer to the novel tactics of their opponents: instead of attacking the Highlander to the front of him, each redcoat went for the exposed side of the man on his right. More than 1000 Scots were killed for the loss of just 50 English under 'bloody butcher' William Augustus, Duke of Cumberland.

2 BUENA VISTA, 1847

Madcap Generalissimo Antonio Lopez de Santa Anna threw away two wars for Mexico, in the second, losing every battle he fought. In the Texas war he used up much men and equipment at the Alamo and San Antonio. Then at San Jacinto in 1836 he set up camp within only a mile or so of the entire Texan army and ordered his troops to take a siesta. His men were routed and Santa Anna was taken prisoner. Later the shrewd Texans released him, knowing he could only do more damage.

In 1847 at Buena Vista the Generalissimo was less concerned with running a battle than collecting some trophies – a few flags and three cannon – to take home as proof of his stunning victories. His dallying lost the whole of north-east Mexico to America. US troops swiftly followed up with routs at Cerro Gordo and Puebla, where the mines carefully laid by the Mexicans all failed to explode. Mexico City fell shortly afterwards and Santa Anna resigned and fled to Venezuela.

3 FORT ROOYAH, 1858

Just after the Indian Mutiny, in April 1858, General Walpole was sent from Lucknow to clear the rebels from nearby Fort Rooyah. Instead he managed to create an astonishing military fiasco. Having marched his men nine miles, the nincompoop general decided not to bother with any reconnaisance, but to discharge his men at the front of the fort.

Inside, the 300 rebels had been prepared to surrender, but changed their minds when they saw the tired British slamming away against the strongest of their defences.

Two companies of British were lost immediately in concealed ditches. Then Walpole made an even worse decision. He ordered a bombardment and sent his heavy guns round to the west. Most of the cannonballs went straight over the fort and killed British troops to the east.

General Adrian Hope did not believe this and asked to see for himself. Told: 'General, this is no place for you, you must lie down,' he decided to ignore the advice. He was immediately shot through the chest.

Walpole rode dejectedly back to camp while, under cover of darkness, the rebels slipped out of the fort and made good their escape.

4 FREDERICKSBURG, 1862

Probably history's worst commander, General Ambrose Burnside reluctantly took command of the Union side after the battle of Antietam. Having marched to the Rappahannock river he waited three weeks for pontoon bridges to arrive from Washington so his men could cross.

When they did cross they were like tin soldiers in a shooting gallery to the Confederates. Yet if Burnside had done any reconnoitring he would have found he could have forded the river easily upstream – the water was only three feet deep.

Having crossed the Rappahannock, Burnside showed some amazing battle tactics when he attacked General Lee's army with two main thrusts at the strongest position in the line.

Charge after charge was blown apart by Confederate artillery dug in the shelter of a stone wall. Burnside destroyed a tenth of his 120 000-strong army – 12 650 men – in the suicide attacks.

Later he had to retreat back across the river and, not surprisingly, was relieved of his command.

5 STORMBERG, 1899

General Sir William Gatacre, a subordinate of the disastrous General Sir Redvers 'Reverse' Buller, decided on novel tactics against the Boers to capture Stormberg Junction: a night march and a dawn attack. His problem was he didn't know where he was going, and managed to leave behind the one man who did know, an intelligence captain.

Having appointed two guides, who were just as lost as he was, Gatacre found himself behind the enemy lines he was trying to meet head on. That might not have been so bad if he had decided on a surprise attack.

As it was Gatacre decided to about-face his army. The Boers took a little time to recover from the shock of being attacked by an army with their backs to them, but they opened fire and charged. After a full scale retreat, Gatacre seemed quite pleased he had got away with just 90 casualties . . . until he realised 633 men had been left behind and taken prisoner. By contrast, the Boers lost just 6 dead and 27 wounded.

6 SPION KOP, 1900

The rocky outcrop with the name that has set soccer grounds alight remains a monument to military ineptitude. General Buller decided that after his army's failure to lift the siege of Ladysmith they would storm this pocket mountain as a morale booster.

Unfortunately he knew nothing about the mountain or the strength of the enemy which lurked there, chose a dark foggy night for the attack and entrusted the mission to a General Talbot-Coke, much troubled with a gammy leg.

Coke's men fought their way to what they thought was the summit; then decided to dig in. Since the mountain was solid rock, they were unable to find much cover.

When the fog cleared next morning the awful truth dawned. They had not reached the summit. They were on a small plateau with Boers looking down on them from three sides.

Despite a 10:1 advantage in guns, Buller's army gave the battling Britons on the Kop pitiful support. They had given covering fire to a neighbouring peak but suddenly decided the Boers on the peak were British, and stopped firing.

Having lost 700 dead and 1000 wounded, Buller's army was forced into its by now customary retreat.

7   TANNENBERG, 1914

Never a commander in the field, Russian general Aleksander Samsonov had something of a shock when he was put in charge of the Russian 2nd Army at the start of World War I. Putting his men in a dangerous echelon behind the 1st Army, he led them into East Prussia but seemed to have little idea of what to do next, or even where the German forces were. He then announced over the radio that 25 August would be a day of rest for his troops and scored another monster own goal by transmitting uncoded messages giving the Germans exact locations for his troops. His army was encircled. 125 000 of them were captured and the Germans said, 'It was like heading stock into a corral.'

Samsonov decided early that his army was finished and rode off to the front to die in battle. Unfortunately he couldn't even get that right, and had to make a less dignified exit by shooting himself in a wood.

8   GALLIPOLI, 1915

In January 1915, the Russian High Command sent a telegram to London asking that the world's greatest sea power should make some demonstration against Turkey. The result was a disastrous own goal which lost 213 980 men their lives and brought down the Liberal government of the day.

It was decided to invade the Dardanelles, storm the peninsula and capture Constantinople. But the naval attack in February without army support (which arrived a month later), achieved little except hundreds of shell holes and the loss of three British battleships. Only three groups of British and French soldiers managed to get ashore, and they never got off the beaches. Meanwhile British commander General Sir Ian Hamilton relaxed on Greek islands or on board battleships.

The dysentery-racked, bogged-down Allied troops were finally evacuated in January 1916.

9 SINGAPORE, 1941

The British colonial mentality was at its most inglorious over the 'impregnable fortress' of Singapore. The world was stunned when the army, navy and air force garrisons so rapidly surrendered to the Japanese. A total of 138 708 British, Indonesian and Australian soldiers were killed or taken prisoner.

Singapore was magnificently defended against a sea attack from the south, but there was virtually no fortification against an attack from the north. Lt. Gen. Arthur Percival, GOC Singapore, repeatedly ignored advice to step up his defences and refused to act until ordered to do so by Churchill.

Two battleships, HMS *Prince of Wales* and *Repulse*, were sent out to sea with no air cover. They were immediately spotted by the Japanese and torpedoed, with the loss of 840 lives.

Even when Singapore was given 30 minutes warning of a Japanese air attack, no planes were sent up. Air force commanders would not believe the Japanese would attack at night. And there were no British tanks on Singapore – it was agreed that Japanese tanks would not be able to move through the jungle. In the event, they moved between the rows of rubber trees as if trundling down a motorway.

10 TOBRUK, 1942

Overconfidence brought a dramatic reverse for the eighth army at Tobruk. British casualties were 35 000 with incalculable losses in firepower and equipment.

Yet the allies started with a 4:1 advantage in tanks, a 3:2 advantage in artillery, and 600 aircraft as opposed to the Germans' 530.

Rommel, decided the Allied generals, could be dealt with at leisure. But while the British tried the same provenly hopeless tactics of full frontal assault, Rommel danced the battlefields like a ballet master, with feints, outflankings, pincer movements and encirclements. He literally ran rings round the Allies and forced the recall of Field Marshal Sir Archibald Wavell, who was replaced by Field Marshal Sir Claude Auchinleck.

There was another decisive factor: Rommel's equipment, though inferior in numbers, was superior in quality: his guns could pierce tank armour while that of the Allies could not.

Officialdom

It was supposed to be 'Europe's most advanced prison'. But it became known instead as 'the jail that locked convicts out'.

The £50 million, mega-security Maghaberry complex in Northern Ireland was completed in 1982 and designed to hold the country's most dangerous terrorists. It was still waiting for its first customers two years later.

A whole series of design faults were found in the buildings. Then men from the SAS, called in to test the jail's defences, found they could break in and out at will.

To add to the problems, the roof of one of the cell blocks collapsed, and Ulster MP Cecil Walker claimed the prison had its own 'built-in escape tunnel.'

Meanwhile, a governor and 60 staff waited patiently for the first 'guests'. Cynics suggested these should have been the men responsible for the project. But the jail's crowning glory was still to be revealed. Some of the security doors had been installed the wrong way round – keeping warders within and prisoners firmly out.

Officials at Australia's national art gallery are still red-faced about their Rembrandt self-portrait. It was first put on show in 1934, but fifty years later, in 1984, experts revealed that the prize painting was a cheap fake.

John Hancock, a traffic warden from West Bridgford, Notts, loved his job. So much so that the man nicknamed 'Bacon Face' wrote 17 000 tickets for parking offences in 15 years.

You would have though his police employers would have been pleased. Not a bit of it. They complained that the meter man's irrepressible pen had choked the files at police headquarters. He was fired.

An industrial tribunal ruled 'Bacon Face' was 80 per cent to blame for his dismissal.

When the Government of Grenada decided the United States was about to launch an invasion in October 1983, they sent an urgent plea to the Foreign Office in London for help.

The Foreign Office didn't get the wire.

Meanwhile a Scandinavian plastics firm in London's West End were a little bemused by a telex in which the Revolutionary Military Council of Grenada presented its compliments then asked them to do what they could to stop a US invasion.

Not a lot, as it turned out.

That's just about matched by the American Space Agency which, in 1969, sent invitations to the Apollo 12 launch to the American Federation of Astrologers instead of the organisation for Astronomy.

Pillar of the judiciary Judge Roy Tasker of Oakland, Kansas, was summing up in court one day in 1982 when two workmen asked the clerk if they could take away the court's 250-year-old grandfather clock for repairs.

The judge agreed. The men bowed to the court and left.

It was a year before anyone realised the clock had been stolen.

Also proving the law can be an ass, the court usher at Plymouth magistrates' court who, in February 1974, volunteered to act as a human 'guinea-pig' while a policeman demonstrated an arm-hold used to restrain prisoners.

Usher Mr Jan Pearce, 64, was later visited in hospital by PC Brian Stables. The policeman broke his arm.

Said Mr Pearce: 'Constable Stables took hold of my left arm and we heard a crack. He asked me if I'd torn my shirt and I said: 'Torn my shirt. You've broken my arm.'

Said PC Stables: 'Mr Pearce was trying to make it as realistic as possible by posing as an uncooperative prisoner and keeping his arm stiff.'

Delays were common at the New York Parking Violations Bureau. People paying their parking fines faced endless queues, delays and frustration.

That is, until the new window opened. This cut waiting time dramatically. The two men who manned it were always courteous, fast and efficient. Customers, in fact, preferred to go to the end window because the officials there were never rude.

It took the people from the Violations Bureau a long time to notice. But finally, in August 1983, they did. The two brothers who manned the end window weren't civil servants at all. They were crooks.

In an amazing 18 months since setting up shop at the bureau they netted a cool £70000. They were only 'rumbled' after motorists going to renew their licences found their parking fines were still on the computer.

The council at East Kilbride, Ayrshire, came up with a brainwave. To aid a campaign of road safety, they would make the town's lollipop ladies light up in the dark.

But as soon as the angry ladies from the town's school crossings tried their new uniforms, they were wanting to use their metal lollipops on the designers.

They said their new kit must have been designed by men with men in mind. They were conspicuous, all right . . . but all motorists could see were illuminated, flashing bosoms.

Mind you, blinkered officials are like the over-officious – they always come unstuck.

In 1981, shortly before the Royal Wedding, a gatekeeper at Royal Ascot failed to recognise Lady Diana Spencer and refused to let her in. He said: 'I'll never make the same mistake again.' (Presumably he'll never be allowed to).

Also in 1981, Wimbledon champion Martina Navratilova rode to the tournament one day on her bike . . . to be refused entry by the gateman. Seventy-nine-year-old Ted Edwards, a deterrent to the unticketed for 20 years, said: 'I just didn't expect to see her at my gate.'

He added with mounting pride: 'I once turned away Bing Crosby. But he didn't have a ticket anyway.'

To most of us officialdom means the civil service. And how nice to see even the loftiest of them can fall flat on their faces.

In August 1983, Cabinet Secretary Sir Robert Armstrong sent a letter to Whitehall's top 40 civil service chiefs urging them to act to stop leaks of classified documents.

You guessed it. His letter was immediately leaked.

Finally, to jail and to the unwatchful eyes of the penal authorities at Fort Lauderdale, Florida.

In December 1983, the 100 employees of Cell Block E became extremely happy after a man with a wooden leg joined them. It took a while to figure out why. Police and prison officers had mounted a thorough search of drug smuggler 'Long Tom' McMurray – but had overlooked one thing. His wooden leg. The artificial limb had been full of cocaine.

After his leg was confiscated but found empty, and McMurray's fellow jailbirds continued acting strangely at coffee breaks, a perplexed prison official lamented: 'The inmates here have been high for a month.'

20 Pitfalls for Politicos and Those in Public Life

Those who serve (or rule) the rest of us do tend to fall into certain traps. Here is Jones's cynical guide to avoiding the perils of public office.

1   WHAT HAPPENED IN THE PAST . . .
Don't let hidden skeletons rattle. Remove all records from university club files; get a signed affidavit from each member of the family and all former romances promising not to blab.

2   PROMISES AND MANIFESTOES
Whatever you do, never make a firm pledge or promises that can be held against you later when there has been a slight shift in your position (i.e. complete U-turn). Remember the politicians' golden rule: always hedge.

3   THE EMBARRASSING QUESTION
Never answer a question directly. Reply in as vague terms as you can or, better still, answer with a question in return. If this fails, cough uncontrollably.

4   COMING CLEAN
Never admit a mistake, a change of mind, or display any hint of conciliation or reasonableness (this is seen as a terrible sign of weakness). Remember useful phrases like: 'I was misinformed,' 'I was quoted out of context,' and 'I really don't think you have understood my position at all.'

5 TIREDNESS
Sign all autographs, kiss all babies' heads, smile for all photographs. Scream, swear, or cry to yourself later in private. Never have 'one for the road'. If you do feel extreme tiredness coming on, phone for a taxi.

6 EXPLETIVES UNDELETED
If you are going to swear, make sure all the microphones are switched off (cf. Richard Nixon, François Mitterrand).

7 ROYALTY
Never leave before, make jokes to, blow your nose or nod off to sleep in front of members of the Royal Family, especially The Queen (cf. Fred Mulley).

8 PHOTOGRAPHS
Do not pose for pictures while pickled, with toddlers clutching ice cream cornets, with kissogram girls or walking at the water's edge, unless you are confident you can walk on it (cf. Neil Kinnock). Do not pose with female impersonators or notorious London gangsters (cf. Lord Boothby and the Krays).

9 ABROAD
When stepping off a plane for one of those tiresome guards of honour/speeches of welcome, get an aide to hold up a board saying in big letters where you are (cf. Ronald Reagan).

10 DIFFERENT LIFESTYLES
Make sure you brush up on local customs. Do not shake hands when the local style is to rub noses; and vice versa. Do not go to Moscow wearing a hat showing you are in mourning (Harold Macmillan) or give a cheery salute (Bobby Kennedy) which is interpreted by your hosts as the rudest gesture in the local repertoire.

11 THE TENDER TRAP
Avoid going to places of great temptation, e.g. mixed saunas, all-women whist drives, tea dances in Leicester Square (cf. Geoffrey Dickens MP). In Iron Curtain countries, when awakened at 1 a.m. by an attractive blonde asking if you would

like a nightcap, ask yourself: could there be some other motive? It's probably all above board; she has probably fallen head over heels for the refined foreign gentleman suffering from jet lag and hiccups and twenty years her senior, but you never know.

12 MISTRESSES AND ILLICIT AFFAIRS

If you do have a mistress, either end the relationship (cf. Cecil Parkinson) or marry her. Do not share mistresses with mafia chieftains (Jack Kennedy) or Soviet diplomats (J. Profumo).

13 BRIBES

If you can't resist taking them, stick to antiques, ornaments, homes, businesses etc., anything you can give back later pleading 'a complete misunderstanding'. Never accept holidays, cash, drink etc., which you cannot return if pressed.

14 HOLIDAYS

Make sure you go somewhere where you are unlikely to be spotted by British holidaymakers (don't go, e.g. to Faro or Benidorm) or you will attract a lot of unwelcome attention. If some international crisis breaks while you are abroad, remember, people will judge your decision whether or not to return to the office at once entirely in the light of how expensive a time you are perceived to be having.

15 SECRET PAPERS

Do not give these to the office junior to photocopy, especially if she has a penchant for dropping brown envelopes off at *The Guardian* (cf. Michael Heseltine).

16 DIRTY TRICKS, RIGGED ELECTIONS, VOTING

Do not bug rivals' offices or try to rig elections. Get a friend to do it for you. Always vote for yourself, just in case no one else does. Try and persuade your friends to turn out too. If in doubt ply them with sherry and drive them there. One more thing: don't try and vote for yourself more than once. There are laws against that sort of thing.

17 LETTERS

Never write letters to members of the public expressing firmly your policy on an issue. When you have shifted your emphasis slightly six months later (i.e. made a complete U-turn) the letter will be resurrected and sent to the *Daily Express* (cf. Denis Healey).

18 SACRED COWS
Never criticise any of these, e.g. Royal Family, National Gallery, Oxfam, Terry Wogan, Battersea Power Station, Boy George.

19 PRIOR ENGAGEMENTS
If you have a sudden diplomatic illness, do not turn up any-where too visible, e.g. the FA Cup Final, Wimbledon, especially with your secretary.

20 DIPLOMACY
Don't use phrases like 'tanning their hides', 'whipping their asses', 'beating their brains to pulp', etc., unless talking about football hooligans or the French. Always talk in non-controversial, boring phrases like: 'I am sure the public will have every confidence in the realistic measures we have taken when fully cognisant, in the fullness of time, with the facts appertaining.' Similarly never describe any place you visit as 'the pits of the earth', 'the slum capital of the Western world', or 'this god-forsaken hole'. The people in the god-forsaken hole will never vote for you again.

☙ 6 ☙

So Who Said Leisure Always Means Pleasure?

Travel Own Goals

Bert Tester and his wife Louie flew 12 000 miles from Adelaide to Wolverhampton in 1971 to be surprise guests at Louie's parents' golden wedding celebrations.

There was just one thing wrong. Their anniversary was in 1972. The jet-set partygoers had arrived twelve months too early.

Forty-four Northern Ireland soccer fans hired a coach from The Sportsman pub in Redditch to go to Wembley to see Northern Ireland play England in May 1983. Then the inevitable truth dawned.

The match was being played in Belfast.

Everything had gone to plan for the opening of the new £1.3 million Sandwell and Dudley station, West Midlands, in May 1984.

British Rail's area manager, Mr Brian Caritt, was there as TV crews, journalists, and the station's first 30 commuters waited for the inaugural, history-making 6.36 to Birmingham.

Sure enough, the train came into view exactly on time and the assembled pioneers prepared to climb aboard.

There was just one problem . . . the driver forgot to stop.

Back to the air, and the pilot on the early Sabena flight from Brussels to Manchester Ringway in May 1983 eased down the flaps, secured the wheels and slowed for touchdown . . . until a call came on the radio: 'You're at the wrong airport.' The plane had to bank sharply and try again. It had attempted to land at the British Aerospace factory at Woodford, nine miles away.

Four years earlier the mistake had been made in reverse, when a USAF plane that should have been giving a demonstration at Woodford gave a dazzling display to bemused tourists and baggage handlers at the civilian terminal.

Visiting Dubrovnik in 1973 the Queen was surprised to find no reception committee was there to greet her. Unfortunately they had all made hot-foot for Titograd, where they had been told her plane would land after being diverted.

Airport chiefs and civic dignitaries turned out in force at Bangkok airport in December 1979, to welcome John Lindsay, former Mayor of New York.

When he landed they whisked him off in a gleaming limousine complete with Thai and American flags and a full military escort.

Photographers worked overtime as he was presented to a full line-up of Thai ministers and foreign diplomats.

Then the truth slowly dawned . . . this wasn't Jack Lindsay, former Mayor of New York. It was Jack Lindsay, the shirt-maker, owner of a small business in Hackney, east London.

Someone had read through the passenger list and jumped to the wrong conclusion.

Even that cannot compare with the astonishing story of Italian Nicholas Scotti, who managed to spend two days in New York thinking it was Rome.

Having lived most of his life in San Francisco, he was not an experienced traveller and when his plane stopped over in New York, Mr Scotti got out thinking he was in Italy.

He was a bit surprised that everyone seemed to speak English, but he put it down to the fact the friendly Romans were doing all they could to help tourists.

A pity they've pulled down all those historic buildings and put up all these skyscrapers, he thought. In the end he didn't really recognise 'Rome' and no matter how he tried, he couldn't find his old neighbourhood.

At one stage Mr Scotti did seek help from a policeman. As if in on the whole charade, the New York cop, also an immigrant, kept our poor hero from finding out the truth. He answered in flawless Italian.

Peter and Lucia Eachus only had eyes for each other as they left the wedding reception and made for their honeymoon hotel.

So much so that, after driving through the night, they found themselves in Scotland instead of their real destination, Devon.

Peter's mistake was only discovered when Lucia asked: 'Is there a Gretna Green near Torquay?' They had turned the wrong way after leaving the M6 for a tea-break.

Did you hear the one about the Irishman who fell asleep in Dublin . . . and woke up in London?

After getting somewhat sozzled at a Dublin disco in August 1983, barman Eddie Fogarty, 18, tried to take a short cut home across the cargo section of Dublin airport. On the way, he decided to take a bit of shut-eye.

When he woke up the next morning he found himself . . . at Heathrow Airport. He had fallen asleep in an Aer Lingus container bound for London.

Dubbed the 'stoned stowaway' by airport police, he was put on the next flight back to Ireland after his parents had promised to meet the £61 fare.

There was some embarrassment at British Airways, the day they flew a planeload of passengers from Manchester to London free of charge.

Cabin staff were supposed to collect £40.50 fare from each of the 130 passengers on the 40 minute shuttle flight. Unfortunately on one memorable journey every one of them forgot.

Absent-minded John Follows, 80, of Corfe Mullen, Dorset, flew 3000 miles to New York in May 1984, to see his daughter. Unfortunately he had to catch the next flight home.

He had forgotten her address.

In 1855, 200 pioneers and railway fans boarded the carriage train making the inaugural run from St Louis, Missouri, to

Jefferson City. It wasn't a good trip – on the way it plunged into the Gasconade River.

Workmen hadn't got round to finishing the line.

Members of Merthyr Tydfil rugby club were all set to fly to Paris for the France v. Wales rugby international in February 1984. But when they arrived at Rhoose, Glamorgan, airport, they began to suspect something was wrong.

They seemed to be the only Welsh supporters flying to Paris . . . while hordes of French rugger fans, for some unknown reason, were just arriving, having travelled the other way.

Yes, the awful truth dawned. The match was being played in Cardiff.

Only marginally more successful was transatlantic yachtsman Ginger Elliott from Poole, Dorset. In the summer of 1983, he braved heavy seas, a broken fuel line and lack of food in a solo voyage to the United States. But disembarking in New York, he was promptly arrested as an illegal immigrant.

Finally, in November 1983, jobless Alan Mattock, 19, stole an ocean-going yacht so he could sail to America in search of work.

He thought his trip would take three days and stocked up with . . . three packets of biscuits and a can of baked beans.

Unfortunately when he took the £20 000 boat *Stowaway* out of Cardiff docks, he took the wrong turn. Instead of veering right, out to sea, he turned left straight up the Bristol Channel. After 20 miles he ran aground and had to be rescued by helicopter.

Placing him on probation at Cardiff magistrates' court, stipendiary Sir Lincoln Hallinan told him it was 'time to get back on an even keel'.

Asked if he would try again Mattock replied 'No, it's too bloody dangerous. Next time I will try to steal a plane.'

Huntin' Shootin' Fishin'

Man's pursuit of wild birds and animals is not without cost. Watch out – the animal empire can bite back.

Stockman Arthur Crosbie, of Tipperary Station, Northern Australia, had the dubious distinction of being shot by a kangaroo. Having wounded the animal with a shot from his service rifle, Mr Crosbie did not want to waste another shot. He pinned the animal down with the butt. The kangaroo had an answer to that. It wrapped its finger round the trigger and pulled hard . . . wounding the astonished hunter in the arm.

Two British countrymen, Louis Murphy and Ralph Slocombe, both had to spend a week in hospital at Barnstaple, Devon, after being shot by their dog. While out hunting, it stood on the trigger of their shotgun and peppered them both with buckshot.

In California, a hunter fired at a flock of geese flying overhead. One plummeted down, struck him full on the head, and put him in hospital for 45 days.

You can see it in the statistics. Figures released by New York State's Department of Environmental Conservation for the 1982–83 season revealed: wild turkeys, 7313; deer, 185 455; black bears, 694; humans, 9.

But it's safer in America than Italy. Recent figures released in Rome showed that in the 1978–79 season, 107 humans were killed and 1000 injured in sporting accidents. The first day of the 1979 season was celebrated by a man mistaking his aunt for a deer and another cheerfully blasting away his nephew.

In August 1984, Tory Party Deputy Leader Lord Whitelaw managed to 'bag' an unusual brace: Farmer Sir Joseph Nickerson and gamekeeper Lindsay Waddell. The Glorious Twelfth itself in 1976 claimed two distinguished victims: Lord and Lady Martin Fitzalan-Howard both found themselves in Catterick Military Hospital undergoing surgery for the removal of shotgun pellets. Stiff upper lip and all, no one would say who had been such a poor shot.

When John, fourth Marquis of Bute (1881–1947), managed to shoot himself, he ended up in better health than before.

Much troubled by stomach pains, one day the Marquis accidentally discharged his gun as he pushed it through a hedge.

The shot took out his appendix. When the wound healed, he had no more stomach ache.

Retired accountant Charles McDonough hooked an enormous pike out of Canada's mighty St Lawrence river. So pleased was he at his triumph, he held up the fish and kissed it.

The pike responded with a message of its own. It turned over, leaped up . . . and bit McDonough on the cheek.

The wound needed seven stitches.

In Suffolk, an angler was found unconscious on the ground after landing an eel. The most slippery of slippery customers had twisted the line around his throat and tried to strangle him. He was revived just in time.

Ken Williams of Cardiff ended up with a highly unusual catch when he went fly fishing with his friend Dave Stowell in May 1977 – several juicy trout . . . and two left ears . . . his own and pal Dave's. Said Ken: 'We couldn't get the hooks out so we had to cut the line and come home with the flies still in our ears.'

Then there was the Irish angler who went after a pike . . . but sank his car. Danny Cullen, 63, explained later he was trying to manoeuvre his old Austin saloon to shine his headlights on his fishing float. But instead one day in December 1983,his car slipped over the edge of a flooded gravel pit at Rickmansworth, Herts, and began sinking.

Non-swimmer Danny of Willesden, north London, managed to slide out of his car and splash his way to safety.

His car was not so lucky. Said Mr Cullen: 'When I go fishing again I think it will be safer to get a mate to drive me.'

Brad Jeffreys of Houston, Texas, landed a catfish in 1970, but it started flopping about in the bottom of his boat. Its tail struck the trigger of a loaded shotgun . . . peppering poor Mr Jeffreys' rear end with pellets.

Faring even worse was woman angler Maria Cista, 56, of eastern Spain, who was actually killed by the fish she had just caught.

Mrs Cista was struggling to free the fish from the end of her line in the amazing accident in June 1983.

The fish suddenly jumped out of her hand and down her throat . . . and choked her to death.

'I've got a biggie,' yelled Eusebio Rodriguez, rock-fishing at Oxnard, California, in October 1978. A sea-bass, barely a foot long, yanked the 31-year-old angler off his boat and he drowned.

Finally one heroic own goal from the hunted. A rabbit in North Dakota jumped three feet to hurl itself into the whirling propellor of a light aeroplane.

The rabbit died instantly but the aircraft – which was going to be used for the spraying of lethal poison to cut down the rabbit population – was out of action for weeks.

In one brave and noble deed, the kamikaze bunny had spared the lives of hundreds of his fellow-rabbits.

8 Undignified Exits

Spare a thought for those whose final own goals – in female company – has brought sniggers from the rest of us.

1   ATTILA THE HUN, AD 453
Years of rape and pillage finally took their toll on the poor old

warrior chieftain who, after marrying for the umpteenth time, and retiring to consummate his vows, was found the next day dead in bed. The version most widely believed is that he burst an artery while over-indulging himself.

2   POPE LEO VIII, AD 965
Not the world's most pious pope, Leo VIII was installed by force after a Roman synod deposed and expelled John XII for insurrection and conspiracy. Leo, regarded by many as an 'antipope' died in 965 of a stroke while committing adultery.

3   FRANZ KOTZWARA, 1793
A Czech musician based in London, Kotzwara, who wrote the sonata *Battle of Prague*, was described by fellow musicians as 'very versatile'. This versatility extended to his private life too, where his favourite sexual practice was to ask young ladies to string him up by the neck and then cut the cord at the last gasping, moment.

In February 1793, in a Vine Street, London, brothel, after years of erotic suspension, he was finally hoist by his own petard and expired. His young female *maîtresse de la corde* Susannah Hill, was tried for his murder but acquitted.

4   FÉLIX FAURÉ, PRESIDENT OF FRANCE, 1899
Poor Mr Fauré is not remembered for his stewardship of France
so much as his ungallant exit from power. Officially, he was
found dead in his office while 'interviewing' a young lady. In
fact, he was found slumped in his specially designed 'sex chair'
after suffering a heart attack during exertions of a strictly
non-political nature.

5   CARDINAL JEAN DANIELOU, 1974
The Vatican said he died of a heart attack in the street but
rumours spread about the colourful demise of the 69-year-old
conservative French cardinal, a strong advocate of celibacy,
whose clothes were in some disarray when his body was discovered in June 1974.

Finally the church had to retract their statement when go-go
dancer Mimi Santoni, 24, whose husband was in jail for pimp-
ing, confirmed press reports that France's leading Jesuit had
been with her in her fourth floor Paris flat when he died.

The church authorities later acknowledged 'certain circumstances' of his death but rebutted suggestions he had broken his
vows of celibacy. They hinted either that he must have been on a
mission to the fallen (he had a record of visiting the premises) or
that the large sum of money he was carrying must have been to
pay off a blackmailer on someone else's behalf.

6   MONSIGNEUR ROGER TORT, 1975
As if the Cardinal had not caused them enough blushes, the
Roman Catholic Church in France were forced to order an
inquiry after the 57-year-old Bishop of Montauban was found
dead of a heart attack in the hallway of a Paris brothel in
January the following year. Reports said he had been 'hurriedly
dressed'. Police said the 'hotel' just off the notorious Rue St
Denis was used exclusively for prostitution. Monsigneur Tort
had been in Paris for a bishops' meeting and stayed at a
charity-run home for priests. When he went out he said he was
going to spend the evening with 'a wartime friend'.

7   NELSON ROCKEFELLER, 1979
Details of the death of the former Vice-President and Governor
of New York State were slow to emerge, but it is clear he died of
a heart attack at his New York town house in discussions of an

artistic nature with a Rubenesque 25-year-old aide, Miss Megan Marshack.

The Rockefeller family were not keen for an inquiry into Rocky's demise, however. There was no autopsy and he was cremated hurriedly. Afterwards there were some fascinating unanswered questions. Why did Miss Marshack call a friend, Ponchitta Pierce, and not the medical services when he suffered his heart attack? What happened in the 'missing' hour between his fatal coronary and the first emergency call? And if, as stated, they were working on a book, why did not papers appear to be around at the time?

Newspaper allegations that Mr Rockefeller 'died while making love' were vigorously denied by his family.

8   JIMMY FEROZZO, 1983

San Francisco night club boss Jimmy 'the Beard' Ferozo died in the most unusual circumstances . . . making love on the lid of a grand piano. One night after the Condor Club closed in November 1983, the night-club romeo began a steamy sex session with 23-year-old stripper Teresa Hill. But as they started to make love on the top of the grand, they accidently triggered a mechanism raising the piano from the floor. As their passion grew, neither of them noticed. The sex romp ended with the couple crushed against the ceiling. After Miss Hill screamed for help, police arrived and she was taken to hospital with bruises. But Ferrozo was already dead.

Hung up on Sex

Vienna's embarrassed police chief found a den of vice where he least expected it – in the city's police training school.

After 60 policewomen were admitted for the first time, in 1966, an investigation showed midnight parties, love games and 'prowess' contests had taken their toll.

The result: instead of 60 ready, willing and able young recruits, tests found more than half of the WPCs . . . 36 of them . . . were pregnant.

In April 1974, wives of workers from the British Leyland car plant staged a 'sex strike' in retaliation for their husbands downing tools at the factory and not bringing home the weekly wage.

In sympathy with the men, a 42-year-old ex-Carmelite nun formerly called Sister Maria, offered to entertain the car workers free of charge at her home in Chesterfield Road, Mansfield, Notts.

But when the first car worker arrived and presented his credentials . . . Sister Maria promptly fainted.

She was stretchered to the casualty department of a local hospital and given tranquillisers.

Afterwards Sister Maria . . . latterly divorced mother-of-three Mrs Emma Smith, said: 'He told me he had driven three hours non-stop to see me. He was very polite and presented his marriage certificate and his union card to show he was genuine.

'But when he produced the rest of his credentials, I just fainted on the lounge floor.'

An ambulanceman who attended said: 'She was badly shocked. She could not say what happened and kept murmuring: "Goodness me, goodness me!" '

Family planning expert Dr Yvonne Hodges, 29, was used to helping women prevent themselves getting pregnant.

But clients at her advice clinic in Axminster, Devon, were stunned in October 1983, when she told them she was expecting . . . and it wasn't planned.

She said after the birth of son Timothy in December: 'There

are ways and means a good deal safer than the one we were using. It just shows we can all make mistakes.'

A couple left the party at Luton's flying club for a rather different form of aerobatics. Silently they climbed into the cockpit of a light aircraft . . . took part of their clothing off . . . and settled down for a sex session.

But they were in for a shock. Unfortunately their every manoeuvre could be seen from the airport control tower, and they hadn't got clearance for that sort of thing. Night watchmen were sent to investigate.

The low level joystick frolics in a six-seater Piper Aztec cost the couple £50 each after they appeared at Luton Magistrates Court in September 1983. Mr David Ward, prosecuting, said: 'They could have damaged the controls.'

They called it the world's greatest sex fair. And they prophesied that anyone who didn't book early would not get a bed.

The week-long festival boasted public shows of sexual inter-course, a night club welcoming 'audience participation' in sex shows, and mixed sauna baths.

One of the first visitors to the 'all join in' night club was 80-year-old local pensioner Jens Hansen who said: 'All my life I've dreamed of this.'

But what was billed as the world's greatest sex fair in March, 1970 was an undignified flop. There were £7000 losses and the townsfolk said: 'This freak show won't be welcome back.'

Another sex fair was organised the following year in the Danish city of Copenhagen . . . but lost £10 000. Instead of the expected 25 000 sex-hungry visitors, only 6000 turned up.

One Dane said: 'People are sick and fed up with sex, sex, sex. They are finding *Love Story* a nice change.'

One of the organisers behind the lewdest of own goals said: 'Our show was too classy.'

French businessman Charles Lebrun, 40, had a novel plan to cure his wife Josephine's 'bedroom headaches'.

He staggered home dishevelled, reeking of scent, and with lipstick on his collar.

She said nothing. But the headaches got worse.

Then one night Charles gave a secretary a lift home from an office party. It was all quite innocent. But she gave him a goodnight kiss.

Snap! Headache Josephine had had her husband followed by a private detective. No, of course she didn't believe him.

She went to live with her mother in Toulouse. He was ordered by a judge in December 1982 to pay £515 a month maintenance.

A Swedish man who gave his wife injections of drugs to increase her sexual performance found his experiment cruelly backfired.

She became so sexually demanding he had to stay off work to satisfy her constant need for sex. And finally he had to steal to pay for more of the drugs to keep up his own strength.

The case of the violently oversexed Swedish housewife was revealed by Dr Donald Louria, president of the New York State Council on drug addiction, in December 1970.

He said there was worse to come . . . the wife eventually left her husband because her sexual appetite was too much for one man – even the most highly sexed – to cope with.

Fort Lauderdale police were astonished by the young couple's predicament, but were sympathetic just the same. The husband explained he and his wife had been 'fooling around' when they had their accident. The real problem came when he had dropped the key. That wouldn't have been so bad if the dog had not gone and eaten it . . .

Yes, that was why they were trapped, red-faced, both completely naked, and handcuffed together.

Al Hamburg of Torrington, Wyoming, promised his mistress his car 'if you make love to me fifty times'. To keep score, he gave her a chart with fifty squares on it.

She, unfortunately, grew tired of the arrangement and after thirty-three lovemaking sessions – some in bed and some in the back of the car – made off with the car anyway.

Unhappy Al lost his case for breach of contract in March 1984, even after the court heard the sad story of how he had no car, no girl – and only thirty-three golden memories.

The amateur dramatic production of *The Last of the Red Hot Lovers* due to be staged at Kingston Bagpuize, Oxfordshire, in November 1983 had to be postponed for a year. The leading lady, Mrs Judy Rusk, 27, became pregnant.

Australian army captain Richard Gibbons of Dee Why, near Sydney, complained to the *Daily Mirror* in February 1984 about his 'night on the town' in London.

He had been to a 'posh dive', he said, where he had spent two hours chatting up a girl singer. Finally he realised he had been wasting his time.

'Ever heard of Marilyn? Well, she's a bloke,' the captain complained. 'You poms are turning out just like we said.'

A worldly-wise wife from Hastings, Sussex, wrote to the *Daily Star* in April 1984, telling how her husband had given the game away that he was having an affair:

'He came home one night the worse for drink, and after half an hour of tossing, turning and grunting, got out of bed, trying to put on his trousers.

' "What are you doing," I asked.

' "I have to go home now," he said.'

A strange story from India in January 1981, and what was claimed as an advance in the treatment of impotence. A Bombay urologist, Dr D. D. Gaur, pioneered a new technique which consisted of implanting rigid silicone tubes into the male sex organ, thus making it permanently erect, but capable of being hinged up or down.

The men fitted with Dr Gaur's 'flexirod penile prosthesis' reported excellent results.

The eleventh was not so happy after he had agreed to the £1700 treatment. For what *Medical News* reported as a 'hang malfunction' meant he had an unusual problem. His prosthesis would just not flex down.

How much this hampered him in his daily routine is hard to say. But according to Dr Gaur, he tucked his organ up against his abdominal wall most of the time and was 'still quite happy'.

In Turin, Italy, in July 1983, bikini-clad Anna Eprica offered to spend the night with the strongest man in the bar. Police had to break up the mêlée that followed, in which six windows, fifty-eight glasses and four chairs were smashed. Not to mention the barman . . . he suffered multiple injuries.

10 Great Own Goalscorers of Modern Times

1   SPIRO T. AGNEW

The former Governor of Maryland and Vice-President under Nixon was a man whose tongue always got him into trouble. What's more, upset by the way his blunt edges were roughed up even further in the media, he decided to take on America's liberal journalists. He lost.

Agnew called Polish Americans 'Polacks', a Nisei reporter 'a fat Jap', and went into the quotation books with 'Once you've seen one ghetto, you've seen them all.'

In October 1967, after allegations surfaced in the press of illegal payments while he was Governor, Agnew pleaded guilty to one specimen charge of income tax evasion on the understanding he would not go to jail. Fined $10,000 and given three years' probation, Agnew was nonetheless thoroughly disgraced and he resigned the Vice-Presidency the same day.

2 GEORGE BROWN

Later Lord George-Brown, the deputy leader of the Labour Party in the 1960s was in his time not only Britain's most colourful politician, but also its most disaster prone. Stories abounded about Mr Brown's wild and sometimes outrageous behaviour. Even before he became Foreign Secretary, he had managed to insult all manner of foreign diplomats. Typical was a cocktail party at the Italian embassy, where he managed to joke about ice cream, remind his hosts who won the last war *and* comment on the standard of Italian soldiery, all in his first two sentences.

Sometimes he went the other way, like shouting 'God Bless Gromyko!' or singing a Wagner aria in praise of the Germans at a time of neo-Nazi revival.

Mr Brown was driven home from London airport by police because he was 'tired'; he cancelled a speech in Wales because of 'an important engagement' which turned out to be the FA Cup Final. '*How does he manage to keep getting away with it,*' wailed John Junor of the *Sunday Express* in November 1967.

Well, eventually, he didn't. Another side to the calamity-courting Mr Brown was his constant offering of his resignation if he didn't get his way. It was always retracted later, of course. But in March 1968, Brown clashed with Premier Harold Wilson and offered his resignation as Foreign Secretary because, he said, Wilson was running the country in 'too presidential a manner'. This time, his resignation was gleefully accepted by the canny Wilson and George Brown was out.

3 JOE CLARK

Mr Clark, who, in 1978, became Canada's first Conservative Prime Minister for 16 years, was one of the most unsuccessful premiers of modern times. Elected with only 36 per cent of the popular vote, he soon found himself in deeper trouble after failing to carry out any of his main election pledges, including one to slash taxes.

Famed for Malapropisms and mixed metaphors, on the stump he gave the press such gems as 'We can beat the Liberals even with one engine tied behind our back,' and 'I don't want to be wrongly nuanced.' He asked a British Columbia miner: 'What is your total productability here?'

But as he fought a distinctly lacklustre second campaign, it was the Joe Clark jokes which finished the wimpish PM. (*Q. Why does Joe Clark carry a turkey? A.* For spare parts.... *First man*: Have you heard the latest Joe Clark joke? *Second man*: But I am Joe Clark. *First man*: Then I'll go very slowly.) Pierre Trudeau was back by a mile.

4   GENERAL DE GAULLE

The President who cried 'wolf' once too often. His favourite tactic was to call a referendum and to ask people to choose between patriotism, duty, loyalty (i.e. to himself) and chaos. In 1958, on a referendum on the constitution of the Fifth Republic, the General got an 80% 'yes' vote. In 1961 he got a 75% 'yes' for self-determination for Algeria; in April 1962, he got a 90% 'yes' vote for Algerian independence; and in October 1962, he got a 62% 'yes' vote for the French presidents to be elected by universal suffrage.

After the riots of May 1968, though the next presidential election was not due until 1972, De Gaulle called another referendum. He promised a new style of 'participatory' government mid-way between communism and capitalism and gave the people the usual choice: himself or chaos. He had asked once too often. He got a 52.4% 'No' vote and was on his way from power.

5   THOMAS A. DEWEY

The one-time Republican Governor of New York scored the biggest own goal in US political history when he lost to Harry S. Truman in the presidential election of 1948. No one could believe it. Pollsters, pundits and the public had all put Dewey way out in front. The only person who believed Truman could win was Truman himself.

Indeed, former attorney Dewey's snatching of defeat from *The Jaws of Victory* (the title of his autobiography) put him in the select band of twice-rejected US presidential candidates.

Dewey fought a truly awful campaign in 1948, believing he only had to show his face to the public to win. He said later he had considered going on the offensive and answering some of Truman's bitter attacks on him. But his aides told him: 'Don't worry. It's only Truman. You can't possibly lose.'

6 GENERAL LEOPOLDO GALTIERI

In the spring of 1982, the Argentine president thought of a novel way of distracting public attention from a deepening economic crisis and increased tension about the 'disappearance' of some 6000 dissidents, believed murdered by government death squads. He decided to invade the Falkland Islands, which were British territory.

Unfortunately the General and the rest of Argentina's military junta read too much into suggestions Britain might acquiesce in such an invasion. Instead Britain sent a task force, and General Galtieri and his troops were given a rather severe bloody nose. Worse was to come for Galtieri, who must by now have wished he had never bothered. Three days after the British victory on June 14 he was ousted, stripped of his rank, jailed for 30 days . . . and ordered to face a full court martial.

7 ED MUSKIE

Senator Edmund Muskie of Maine scored an even more spectacular presidential own goal when, while Democratic frontrunner in 1972, he did an amazing self-destruct in the New Hampshire primary by breaking down in front of the TV cameras and weeping uncontrollably.

It was a 'dirty trick' by Nixon supporters that brought it about, though they could hardly have expected such instant and dramatic results. A fake letter in the *Manchester Union Leader* accused Muskie of laughing at a description of French Canadians ('Canucks') as New Hampshire blacks.

After a gruelling day's campaigning Muskie went down to the newspaper's offices for a confrontation. He broke down in tears. It looked a terrible sign of weakness in a man who aimed to lead the West. He said: 'It was a bitch of a day. I just got goddammed mad and choked up over my anger.'

8 GEORGE OLDFIELD

Assistant Chief Constable (Crime) for West Yorkshire Police during the hunt for the Yorkshire Ripper, Mr Oldfield managed to throw everyone off the scent in the summer of 1979 by presiding over a series of press conferences at which he insisted the mass killer of young girls had a 'Geordie', or north-eastern, accent.

Hoax tape 'confessions' had been sent from Wearside and police throughout the country were told to eliminate from their inquiries anyone who did not have a Geordie accent. It was a terrible error which prolonged the hunt for the killer.

When Peter Sutcliffe from Bradford was eventually trapped in a routine car check in Sheffield, it was revealed he had been interviewed several times: a note in a dead prostitute's handbag was traced to just four firms in the Shipley area; Sutcliffe's car tyres matched prints found at the scene of one killing; and he was a known frequenter of red light districts. His face and moustache matched police 'photofits'.

West Yorkshire police did not use a computer, and the tell-tale signs which should have pointed to the killer never surfaced together. Mr Oldfield suffered a heart attack during the hunt, and for a time was transferred to less arduous duties in charge of traffic.

9   JOHN PROFUMO

Jack Profumo was the British War Minister (as his department was more appropriately called before being restyled the Ministry of Defence) who became, in March 1963, the archetypal major political figure who threw it all away for a sordid affair. The object of his lust was a 19-year-old prostitute on the fringes of the underworld named Christine Keeler. The Profumo affair became one of the scandals of the century and was instrumental in the Conservative defeat of 1964. What made Profumo's own goal so awful was (1) he shared Miss Keeler with, among others, the assistant Soviet naval attaché in London, Commander Yevgeny Ivanov; and (2) he lied to the House of Commons with a denial of 'any impropriety' in his relationship with Miss Keeler. Within hours, he was forced to admit his deception. Resignation and disgrace swiftly followed.

10   DAVID STOCKMAN

Ronald Reagan's financial whizz-kid, who zoomed in from nowhere to become US Budget Director in 1980, aged 35, lost much of his fizz with some disastrous blabbing to the press. In 1981, at his confirmation hearings, he told Congressmen that Reaganomics weren't like Thatchernomics – British Conservative economics had done a sharp U-turn, he said, but US policy would not.

Stockman promised tax cuts, increased growth, and a balanced budget. Within two years the Reagan programme itself had done a sharp U-turn – taxes were raised, and the budget deficits were some of the largest ever seen.

As if this was not a big enough own goal. Stockman contributed one of the most wildly indiscreet magazine interviews ever when, in the autumn of 1981, he told a writer from *Atlantic Monthly* that Reaganomics weren't working, tax cuts had been 'a Trojan horse to bring down the top rate', and 'no one really understands what's going on with all these numbers'. The interview was printed in full, and though he clung on to his job, Stockman's reputation hit a predictable low.

In 1983, another Stockman gaffe surfaced. Unguarded remarks about how he had played President Carter in election TV debate rehearsals 'using a pilfered copy of the briefing book he was going to use' launched the 'debategate' scandal.

7

Don't Ever Leave Anything to the Experts . . .

Commercial Heartbreak

An American firm built a massive factory on a remote Mexican riverbank, for processing pineapples. They thought they could cut costs by sending millions of tins out from there on giant barges. But they hadn't asked about the rainy season. At pineapple harvest time the river flooded its banks. The barges couldn't get near the factory and the firm – left looking right chunks – lost millions.

Then there was the Thermofax copier. It seemed to duplicate very well. Thousands were sold before the firm addressed itself to a rather serious problem: after a few weeks, its copies turned black and illegible in the files.

You know what they say: there's always room in the marketplace. If someone could design a better mousetrap, people would buy it. An American did design a better mousetrap. Smart and reusable, at seven cents rather than three, it was cost-saving for anything over two mice. Nobody bought it. What the firm had overlooked was nobody wants a reusable mousetrap . . . they would rather throw the whole thing away than have the unpleasant task of removing a squashed rodent.

The business world is full of such traps for the unwary.

Way back in the 1870s, Joseph Wilson Swan invented an impressive array of electric light bulbs. But everybody now associates the light bulb with Edison.

All Swan's bulbs were technical masterpieces but overly complicated and unsuitable for mass production.

The cannier Edison put himself in the position of the power companies, asked: 'What do they want?' and kept it simple.

He became a multi-millionaire and a legend. Nobody spared much of a thought for poor old Swan.

Some of the all-time great business own goals concern the all-time great 'fab four', the Beatles.

There was their one-time manager Alan Williams, who gave them up as 'rubbish' and told John Lennon: 'You'll never work again.'

Don Rowe, the Decca boss who turned them down with: 'To be frank, Mr Epstein, we don't like your boys' sound. . . . Groups of guitarists are on the way out.'

There was the leader of Howie Casey and the Seniors, who in 1960 pleaded from Hamburg with the agent: 'Don't send them. They're so bad, they'll spoil it for the others.'

Jay Livingstone, head of America's Capitol Records, who said: 'We don't think the Beatles will do anything in this market.'

But finally there was supposedly super-shrewd business brain Brian Epstein himself.

In 1963, he was besieged with offers for endorsements – Beatles T-shirts, wigs, toys, posters, pillows. But for once his business sense deserted him. He thought there was no money in it.

When the man he'd given 90% of the merchandising rights to, Nicky Burne, gave him his first cheque for $9700, Epstein said: 'That's great. I suppose I owe you 90 per cent of this.'

'No,' explained Byrne with a grin. He had taken his cut – $87,300.

It was reckoned Epstein's rare business blunder cost the Beatles more than £50 million.

Mind you, commercial acumen and music don't often go hand in hand. One musician drove five London opera companies to bankruptcy before turning to serious composing, which he was rather better at.

He was continually overspending budgets to try and lure top international stars, and even massively-subsidised companies he ran ended up down the chute.

Finally, in 1733, he grew bored with all the financial foul-ups and started to write oratorios.

His name: George Frederick Handel. Among his subsequent works: *The Messiah*.

When Parker Bros in the United States were first sent something called 'Monopoly' – eventually the world's biggest selling board game – they rejected it, saying it had '52 fundamental errors'.

Irwin Schiff wrote the 1983 American bestseller *How Anyone Can Stop Paying Income Taxes*. Within months the taxman was after him . . . with a bill for $200 000.

Canteen worker Shirley Hill upset her bosses at the Frome, Somerset, factory of Cuprinol Limited, leading producers of wood preservatives, when her heel went through two floorboards in January 1984.

Workers found the floorboards had wet rot.

In the fast lane of the business world is of course the advertising industry, and the ad-men have been responsible for some stunning own goals.

Remember the series of TV ads showing Leonard Rossiter pouring drink over Joan Collins? But do you remember what they were advertising? There's the rub.

In March 1983, the makers of Cinzano switched their account from Collett, Dickinson and Pearce to Foot, Cone and Belding. Said the *Daily Express*: 'Everybody roared with laughter at Leonard pouring the sticky drink over Joan, but no one could remember the sticky drink. Most people questioned thought that it was Martini.'

Meanwhile headache cure Exedrin, advertised in the US by David Jansen, actually had made *twice* as many people think about its biggest rival, Anacin.

There have been worse advertising boners. Ad copy does not travel well, or at least not with some translators.

The slogan 'Come Alive with Pepsi' did big things for American teenagers but the slogan transferred to posters all over Germany lost a little of its gaiety. It read: 'Come alive out of the grave with Pepsi.' Another overseas version promised: 'Pepsi brings your ancestors back from the dead.'

It is to be hoped they won't make the same mistake with the new Vauxhall hatchback, but a while ago General Motors couldn't understand why their Chevrolet Nova sold so slowly in South America. Someone did tell them in the end. 'No va' in Spanish means 'Won't go'.

Hunt Wesson Foods' canned pork and beans became 'Big John's' in Britain, but in 1972 the ad people wanted something catchy and macho for the French-Canadian market. They came up with 'Gros Jos' which sounded fine until a French-speaking adman saw the almost complete campaign. All was scrapped after he pointed out the colloquial translation was 'Big tits'.

Though an even larger advertising boob was made by Smirnoff vodka in 1975. An ad had shown a sultry eastern maiden and the copyline: 'I thought the Kama Sutra was an Indian Restaurant until I discovered Smirnoff.'

Said a dejected Mr Ambler of Smirnoff: 'We made a survey and found that 60 per cent of people did think it was an Indian restaurant.'

While on tales of the unexpected, a strange case of blushes amongst the bosses at Huntley and Palmer, biscuit manufacturers by appointment to HM the Queen and the Queen Mother.

A picture on tins for the Christmas market was a dignified and tranquil one showing an old-fashioned tea party in an English country garden.

It seemed just the thing for granny, said one writer. But if she had looked hard at the picture she would probably have choked on her custard creams.

Just to the rear of two elegant ladies pictured genteely supping tea were two terrier dogs doing something which would have upset even the trendiest of country vicars.

And across the lawn flailed the naked limbs of a young couple definitely not just there for the polite chit-chat.

Huntley and Palmer said it must have been an agency artist's idea of a practical joke. They sent the rest of the 'too hot' tins off to be melted down.

Firms can be the victims of the most appalling bad luck, of course.

When the Ford Motor Company of Australia introduced a new model, the Falcon, they took elaborate steps to make sure no one got a sneak preview.

A month before the car was unveiled, 50 of the new cars were carefully put aboard a string of double-deck railway trucks at Brisbane for the first stage of the journey to leading Sydney showrooms.

It was bad enough that no one had tried to cover them up with tarpaulin, but then disaster struck as the trucks were carefully shunted into their main rival manufacturer's yard to hook up some more wagons.

From their office windows, the rival executives were treated to an unexpected grandstand preview of Ford's 'secret' new model.

How does it feel to drop a giant business brick? Coin expert Raymond Sancroft-Baker, a junior at Christies', London, turned down an offer to buy two wooden figures from Easter Island for £30.

A friend of his bought them instead for a knockdown £10 and he sent them to Christies' for valuation. They were, in June

1983, discovered to be rare early nineteenth century carvings and sent for auction. They fetched £93 000.

Said a sanguine Mr Sancroft-Baker: 'I've not lost any sleep over it.'

In June 1984, an official of New York's immigration department had what he thought at first was a routine request from three Nigerian businessmen to locate a suitable demolition, haulage and shipping firm. But when he heard their full story, he decided to call in the fraud squad.

'It's so we can take home the Statue of Liberty,' they said. 'We bought it for $100 000 from an American visiting our country last January.'

In July 1983, a San Francisco store put on the shelves 18 bottles of wine marked at just over $3 apiece.

Ten of the bottles were 1951 Château Lafite-Rothschild valued at $90 each, the remaining eight were 1966 Château Latour and worth around $120 a bottle.

The store found out their mistake . . . but too late. A wine-loving waiter, Robert Kendall, told them he much liked their special offer, but not until after he had bought every available bottle.

Bank officials at Traverse City, Michigan, had some explaining to do when, in December 1976, they gave a 31-year-old antique dealer's son a bumper Christmas present: they paid him $40 000 for a worthless German 100 000 mark note.

The note had been issued in 1923, in days of hyperinflation, and at the exchange rates prevailing at the time – 4.2 trillion marks to the dollar – was worth less than one American cent.

But when a money dealer called up the National Bank and Trust Company on Stephen Holcomb's behalf and asked how much 100 000 marks was worth, no one bothered to query the date.

They paid up happily at a rate of 39 cents to the mark.

The bank did not press any criminal charges, but sued to try and get their money back. They had trouble.

Holcomb had gone on a massive spending spree buying a

Scout car ($7000), pistol, shotgun, and fishing rod, before jetting off to Chicago 'to have a good time'.

Setting himself up in one of the Windy City's best hotels he got rid of much of his windfall within hours, even tipping an elevator operator $900.

When he returned to Traverse City, detectives impounded his car and made him sign over what was left of the money.

Finally, two cautionary tales suggesting executives should mind their own business.

In January 1983, Mr Geoffrey Marlow, a vehicle alarm expert, had an unfortunate theft from his Northampton home. His car was stolen from the driveway.

And in January 1984, a firm making security devices in Kingsbridge, Devon was robbed of four burglar alarms. The building had no alarm system.

Business Boomerangs

'It is a project which, as far as I can see, has a viable marketing opportunity ahead of it,' said Mr Giles Shaw, Northern Ireland Minister of Commerce, in July 1979, on the car nobody wanted to buy, the De Lorean.

'BRANIFF MEANS BUSINESS' proclaimed a huge advertisement in *The Times* on 13 May 1982. Unfortunately, the airline had folded the night before.

'The Concorde should produce a positive return on investment,' said a TWA study of the supersonic plane in 1968.

How often have business hopes soared sky high, only to crash back to earth with a thud.

> I will conduct a symphony orchestra. I will write the score and the authorities in Britain will have to play under my baton.
>
> *Insurance swindler Emil Savundra*
> *before his Fire, Auto, Marine*
> *company folded leaving 45 000*
> *motorists with no cover*

With his large offices in Regent Street, W1, and Crickle-wood, N.W., staff of 1300, four hundred salesmen, weekly wage bill of £40 000, private plane and £400 000 yacht, John Bloom is clearly here to stay.

> *Donald Zec*, Daily Mirror, *February 1964, on the washing-machine whizz-kid. He went bust four months later*

Mind you, people are never very receptive to innovation.
Electric light will never take the place of gas.

> *Werner Von Siemens, engineer and inventor, 1890*

Radio has no future.

> *Lord Kelvin, Victorian physicist*

It can be exploited for a certain time as a scientific curiosity, but apart from that it has no commercial value whatsoever.

> *August Lumiere on his invention, the moving picture projector*

Even Walt Disney was once told by his marketing men when contemplating a film called *Snow White and the Seven Dwarfs* – later a classic:
No audience will ever be able to take more than ten minutes of animation.

Said the Remington Arms Company on being offered the rights to an invention called the typewriter:
No mere machine can replace a reliable and honest clerk.

And so it went on.
The airship probably has many years of life – perhaps at least 50.

> *Sir Sefton Brancker, designer of the R101 (he died when it crashed at Beauvais, France, in 1930)*

We shall never get people whose time is money to take much interest in atoms.

> *Samuel Butler*

Television won't last. It's a flash in the pan.
Mary Somerville, educational radio
presenter, 1948

In all likelihood world inflation is over.
Managing Director of the
International Monetary Fund, 1959

Take Lord Sainsbury. Typical establishment. A lot of
people in his position said I'd be broke in three weeks. Well
I've proved them wrong.
John Bloom, February 1964
But not, alas, for long.

The Worst Laid Schemes

The world of science and technology, and planning – where
accuracy is so vital that one decimal point out of place, one
badly taken reading, one overlooked snag, can cost millions – is
one which positively invites disaster.

In July 1962, Mariner 1, NASA's first probe to take a close
look at Venus, was launched from Cape Canaveral. As the
spacecraft separated from its booster rocket, Mariner suddenly
veered off course. Launch officials were forced to push a button
destroying both rocket and spacecraft.

Later it was revealed a programmer had omitted a minus sign
from data fed into the launch computer. The simple mathematical error cost the US taxpayer more than $18 million.

Going back a little in time, George Stephenson was the un-
doubted father of steam traction. But really that title should
have gone to Cornish inventor Richard Trevithick, if he had not
been such a poor planner.

As far back as 1801, he unveiled his 'Puffing Devil' coach.
This unfortunately broke down, and while himself repairing at a
nearby inn, Trevithick forgot to put the engine's fire out. The
boiler burst, and that was the end of the 'Puffing Devil'.

Trevithick's second steam engine took the road in 1803; he
tried to drive it to London, far too long a distance, and that
broke down as well.

In 1808 he brought a 'steam circus' to Euston Square which included a steam railway engine. This time one of the wheels broke loose, the loco overturned, and the show had to be abandoned.

Trevithick could have been a national figure and a multi-millionaire. As it was after a spell in Peru, where he managed to become embroiled in the civil war, he returned to London to die penniless.

Another great engineer who was not without his disappoint-ments was Isambard Kingdom Brunel.

His 322ft *Great Britain* may have pioneered the modern liner but it couldn't raise steam. Its engines were underpowered and on only its fifth voyage on September 1846, the great steamship ran ignominiously aground in Dundrum Bay, Ireland.

His 600 ft *Great Eastern* was again bedevilled by delays, and on its way from the Thames builders' yard to Holyhead in 1859 suffered an explosion at Hastings in which five died. She was eventually used as a cable layer before being broken up in 1899.

But Brunel's greatest own goal was the Broad Gauge. While every other railway company in Britain had settled on the Newcastle coal companies' 4ft 8½ins gauge, Brunel dismissed it as the coal wagon gauge and conceitedly carried on with his 7ft gauge, 'a gauge more commensurate with the mass and velocity to be attained'. His costly stubbornness ended after 54 years in May 1892 when the broad gauge was torn up and the Great Western Railway joined its rivals. It was the biggest – and most unnecessary – modernisation of railway history.

Of many who perished trying to pioneer manned flight perhaps we should mention Otto Lilienthal, the German engineer who developed the glider with his brother Gustav. His was typical of the spirit of the early aviators. Strapping himself to a pair of wings and jumping off a hillock, Lilienthal made more than 2000 flights in five years before the inevitable happened.

One day in August 1896, a sudden gust of wind caught his flying machine and he crashed to the ground. His last words summed up the heroic foolhardiness of the times: 'We have to make sacrifices,' he panted as he expired.

In March 1967, the *Torrey Canyon*, a 120 000 ton tanker fully laden with crude, went aground off the Scillies spewing forth an oil slick 35 miles long and 15 miles wide. It took rather too long to realise there had been an environmental disaster of epic proportions.

OWN GOAL ONE came when 160 000 lbs of bombs dropped over three days by Royal Navy Buccaneers and RAF Hunters failed to sink the tanker or dispose of the slick. Instead they only managed to create heavy atmospheric pollution as well as that to the sea.

OWN GOAL TWO came with a massive operation to save fish and sea birds using 2.5 million gallons of detergent. A subsequent report found that the vast expanse of detergent had killed more wildlife than the oil.

Another giant blunder by the British government was the £14 million oil platform yard at Portavadie, Loch Fyne. It was hastily built in 1976 during the North Sea oil boom but by July 1983 had not received a single order.

The expensive white elephant included a dry dock 100 ft deep and a 25-acre village to accommodate a non-existent workforce.

The original planning permission stipulated the yard had to be filled in once work was finished, and in 1983 work began returning Loch Fyne to its original state. This was due to swallow up at least another £1 million of taxpayers' money.

The giant multi-shell structure of Sydney Opera House was an instant hit as an Australian national emblem but as a story of planning failures it took some beating.

The inside of the Opera House had to be completely redesigned with the main opera theatre drastically reduced in size (making it the smallest opera house in the world). The escalation in cost was itself a world record – soaring from an original 7 million to 102 million Australian dollars.

And there still wasn't room for a proper car park.

Engineers followed the plans for the Bogota to Guirardota railway in Colombia to the letter. They started work from both ends, gradually working towards the middle.

Sure enough, they met at exactly the designated point, on the designated day.

There was just one problem. The two sets of workmen had been using different gauges.

In Moscow, in December 1983, a new optical centre opened with all the latest ophthalmic equipment and a large staff of fully-trained oculists. The showpiece centre was hailed as a great breakthrough in making quick and accurate assessments of people's need for spectacles. There was just one little thing. . . . Due to a shortage, there were no spectacles in Moscow – though more were expected in a couple of years or so.

In December 1983, the space shuttle *Columbia* with its $1 billion cargo, the European *Spacelab*, faced an unscheduled extension of its flight after No 1 and No 2 computers both shut down.

At one point both stopped at the same time and nothing was steering the orbiter.

One of the worst problems for the astronauts, however, was something rather more basic. Wind.

Hydrogen gas accumulated so much in the shuttle water supply that, on behalf of the flatulent threesome, pilot John Young said: 'We're all right up here, just as long as no one lights any cigarettes.'

Not in Your Lifetime or Mine

'What can you consider more silly and extravagant than to suppose a man racking his brains, and studying night and day how to fly?' said William Law.

'The atomic bomb will not go off and I speak as an expert in explosives,' Admiral William Leahy told President Truman in 1945.

'Television won't matter in your lifetime or mine,' wrote Rex Lambert, editor of *The Listener*, in 1936.

No wonder science is the mother of invention – more the invention by scientists of excuses to explain why they were wrong.

When the pioneer of the jet engine, Sir Frank Whittle, took his designs to the professor of Aeronautical Engineering at Cambridge University he was told: 'Very interesting, Whittle, my boy – but it will never work.'

Even the father of the greatest scientist of all, Charles Darwin, had this to say to his offspring: 'You care for nothing but shooting, dogs, and rat catching, and you will be a disgrace to yourself and all your family.'

It would be found altogether useless in practice, because the power being applied in the stern, it would be absolutely impossible to make the vessel steer.

Sir William Symonds, surveyor of HM Navy, 1837, on propellor driven ships

I must confess that my imagination, in spite even of spurring, refuses to see any sort of submarine doing anything except suffocating its crew and floundering at sea.

H. G. Wells, 1902, just a decade before the U-boats

The aeroplane will never fly.

Lord Haldane, 1907

X-rays will prove to be a hoax.

Lord Kelvin, Victorian physicist

There is no likelihood that man can ever tap the power of the atom.

Dr Robert Millikan, 1923

Atomic energy might be as good as our present day explosives, but it is unlikely to produce anything very much more dangerous.

Winston Churchill, 1939

I do not believe in the probability of anything very much worse than mustard gas being produced.

Professor J. B. S. Haldane, 1937

Relativity is the moronic brain child of a mental colic. Voodoo nonsense. By 1940, the relativity theory will be considered a joke.

George Francis Gillette, 1929,
promoter of the rival 'Backscrewing
theory of gravity!'

Einstein has not a logical mind. Sometimes one feels like laughing. And sometimes one feels a little irritated that such a hodgepodge can be seriously accepted anywhere for thought.

Very Rev. Jeremiah J. Callaghan,
president of Duquesne University,
Pittsburgh

I cannot see any nation or combination of nations producing the money necessary to put up a satellite in outer space or to circumnavigate the moon.

Astronomer Royal Sir Richard
Woolley, 1957

30 Ways to Commit Professional Hara-Kiri

1 Get the boss's daughter pregnant.
2 Get the boss's wife pregnant.
3 Worst of all, get the boss's mistress pregnant.
4 Order yourself a bigger desk than the boss's.
5 Come to work in a bigger car than the boss, then pinch his parking space.
6 Tell the boss you don't like his tie.
7 Tell the boss you don't like his shoes.
8 Tell the boss how bald he's looking.
9 Earn so much commission, you're being paid more than the boss.
10 Come to work dressed like a punk.
11 Come to work dressed like Boy George.
12 Come to work dressed like Liberace.
13 Forget to mail the boss's board meeting minutes.
14 Forget to mail the boss's golf club subs.

15 Forget to mail the boss's football pools.

16 When the boss says 'I want you to tell me what's wrong with this company,' tell him the truth.

17 Bluffing 'I've just been offered a job by our rivals' when trying to get a raise. (This invites the instant response: 'You can pick up your cards this very afternoon'.)

18 Submit extravagant plans showing how the office could function just as well with one person less. (The one person less will be you.)

19 Take time off for more than six grandmothers' funerals in any three month period (that's stretching it a bit).

20 Drink dry the boss's secret filing cabinet.

21 Set off the sprinklers and accidentally flood the building.

22 Set off the sprinklers and deliberately flood the building.

23 Wipe everything off the office computer while trying to play chess challenge.

24 Wipe everything off the office computer while trying to play space invaders.

25 Wreck more than three office cars in one calendar month.

26 Convert your office Marina into a V-16 customised hot-rod dragster.

27 Keep the key to the storeroom all afternoon when one of the directors wants it for an important executive discussion with his secretary.

28 Be seen on TV in the crowd at Wimbledon on the day of your grandmother's funeral.

29 Admit to personal failings, e.g., you were the one who wrecked the £12 million Brazil deal.

30 Make the boss's holiday arrangements and send him to the wrong airport.

8

The Whole World's a Stage . . . so Let's Hope No One's Watching

Showbiz Own Goals

'She's just not different enough,' pop singer Lulu pronounced on a young upstart from Scotland, Sheena Easton, in 1980.

'If they get anywhere, it will have to be without the vile-looking singer with the tyre tread lips,' said the producer on the first TV appearance of the Rolling Stones.

'That boy has no talent whatsoever,' said André Charlot to Beatrice Lillie about Noel Coward.

The entertainment world is renowned for its chickens coming home to roost.

In 1984, the latest TV blockbuster from America reached Britain – *The Thorn Birds*. Never has one show been so unanimously and derisively panned by the critics.

Under the headline 'HOLLYWOOD BIRD LAYS A BIG EGG', Hilary Kingsley wrote in the *Daily Mirror*: 'The only things wrong with *The Thorn Birds* are the story, the script, the acting, the settings and the pace. Apart from that it's great. And I bet there isn't a performance this year to match Rachel Ward as Meggie – for awfulness, that is.'

'Tepid – another Dallas, only with more funerals,' wrote Katherine Hadley in the *Daily Express*.

'I didn't realise it was a comedy show, Monday's episode was hilarious,' wrote Stafford Hildred in the *Daily Star*.

But the British public gave their own rather solid thumbs down . . . to the critics. For one episode, the show attracted so many viewers – 22 million – it brought a surge of electricity of

2200 megawatts, more than for the Royal Wedding, and an extra power station had to be brought into operation.

Hilary Kingsley claimed 'The Thorn Bird has laid an egg – the biggest for years.' No, dear Madam, I think you did.

Those supposedly 'in the know' in the entertainment world are famed for getting it wrong, of course.

A BBC executive told journalist Frances Coverdale she would have to get the gap between her two front teeth filled if she was going to make it as a newscaster.

When they did deign to let Ms Coverdale appear, she was an instant hit with the viewers. Toothy smile and all.

The world's most powerful critic, Clive Barnes of the *New York Times*, dropped a boo-boo when he went to see a show in London called *Oh Calcutta!* Mr Barnes slammed it and said: 'It's the kind of show to give pornography a bad name.' *Oh Calcutta!* ran for *ten years*.

One big Hollywood producer not renowned for his diplomacy, shot down the ambitions of one young actress in just twelve words: 'Ya never gonna be a star, kid – ya just ain't pretty enough.' He told her to get a job as a waitress.

Pamela Sue Martin went on to fame and fortune as Fallon Carrington in *Dynasty*.

When the Australian pop group *Men at Work* gave their first concert in London in December 1982, one well-known music critic said their performance was 'incredibly loathesome'. Another wrote: 'They are about as lively as a dead wombat.'

They went on to be the most successful group of 1983, winning a US 'grammy' for best new artists, selling more than six million copies of their debut album, and topping the charts in Britain and the US with their single '*Down Under*'.

Talking of the pop charts . . . writer, broadcaster and musician Benny Green was working for the *New Musical Express* when the editor asked him about a new idea . . . listing the week's best-selling records in order of popularity, making a 'Top Twenty'.

Said Green later: 'I was so amazed that anyone should bother with such a daft idea that I asked the editor what his game was.'

Jack Nicholson is an actor who has certainly dropped a few bricks in his time.

He could have played the lead role in *The Great Gatsby* (finally acted by Robert Redford), but refused to work with Ali McGraw. A pity – she didn't appear in the film.

He could have had one of the three lead parts in *The Sting* but left it to Robert Redford again, plus Paul Newman and Robert Shaw.

Nicholson hero-worshipped Marlon Brando and was thought a natural for the major young role in *The Godfather*. He pulled out when he was told he and Brando would not share a single scene.

Some other famous star-role refusals:

BETTE DAVIS: Turned down Scarlett O'Hara in *Gone with the Wind* because she didn't want to work with Errol Flynn. He wasn't in the film.

GEORGE RAFT: Turned down Humphrey Bogart's three classic parts in *High Sierra* (1941), *The Maltese Falcon* (1941) and *Casablanca* (1942).

HEDY LAMARR: Turned down Ingrid Bergman's female lead in *Casablanca*. She didn't want to work with an incomplete script.

NOEL COWARD: Turned down Dick Rodgers' offer to direct and star in *The King and I*. 'A waste of time,' said Coward.

MARY MARTIN: Turned down the lead role of Eliza Doolittle in the stage show *My Fair Lady*. She said that composers Alan Jay Lerner and Frederick Loewe had lost their talent.

BURT LANCASTER: Turned down Charlton Heston's Oscar-winning lead role in *Ben-Hur* (1959).

JACK LEMMON: Turned down *The Hustler* (1960), a monster hit for Paul Newman.

WILLIAM HOLDEN: Turned down Gregory Peck's famous role in *The Guns of Navarone* (1961). He asked for – and didn't get – $750 000 and 10 per cent of the gross.

√ KIRK DOUGLAS:　Turned down the lead role in *Cat Ballou* (1965). Lee Marvin substituted and won an Oscar.

But who'd back an actor's judgment? Warren Beatty told how he met the Hollywood legend Sam Goldwyn in April 1968, and how Goldwyn, then 88, told him: 'You know who I think is going to be President? This young man Richard Nixon.'

Said Beatty: 'I said to myself, that's it. That's it for Sam. Senility has finally hit him if he thinks that Richard Nixon has any chance for the Republican nomination.'

A more obvious gaffe was that committed by actor-comic Jack Douglas. Before his debut on America's *Ed Sullivan Show*, the live network biggie that can make or break international stars, he was given a special dinner at a plush Manhattan eatery.

After being proposed a toast by the powerful Mr Sullivan, Douglas rose to his feet smartly. He was horrified to see crockery and food cascading into important laps.

He had zipped the tablecloth into his trousers.

It's tough being a macho man. At the beginning of *Rebel Without a Cause* James Dean punched a desk with his fist. It was certainly realistic. He broke two fingers.

BBC TV consumer watchdog Chris Serle became famous warning the nation to be on their guard against con-men and business tricksters.

But within weeks of presenting a *That's Life* special on cowboy builders, poor Chris was stung for £5000 ... by cowboy builders.

Another BBC man left with egg on his face was pop producer David Croft.

In 1980 he sent back a tape with a polite rejection to a young singer called George O'Dowd. Within eighteen months, 'Boy George' and his band Culture Club had taken the charts by storm.

Disc jockey Pete Murray was credited with second sight when he wrote the script for the Epilogue for Thames TV in October 1983. His little bedtime chat was called *Coping with Failure*.

'If you are in the public eye, the measure of success and failure is there for all to see,' said Murray.

'In our business you get so used to failure, you are inclined to forget any success you may have had.'

He added: 'Faith restores your confidence when worldly failure threatens to destroy it.'

Mr Murray was certainly tempting fate. Hours before the programme was shown, he was ignominiously sacked from his disc jockey shows on Radio 2.

Did you hear about the BBC film crew that went to Sierra Leone in 1975 to film a series of documentaries?

It was revealed that the BBC men paid white extras five times more than their black counterparts.

Title of their series: *The Fight Against Slavery*.

Finally, two memorable gaffes:
STING who tried to tell a shocked German audience in Augsburg how hot he was. 'Ich bin warm,' he said. His fans were puzzled. To them, he was saying 'I am gay.'

DUSTIN HOFFMAN. End of the line for presentation to Princess Margaret at the Royal Command Performance of

Kramer v Kramer in 1980, the diminutive star decided to make light of things. 'You don't have to talk to me,' he said. 'You must be very tired.'

Princess Margaret agreed. After a cursory greeting, she spun on her heel and sauntered off.

All Phoney and False

'I'm going to be bigger than the Beatles,' said Irish two-hit wonder Crispian St Peters in 1966, just before a rapid descent into oblivion.

'I never knew a guitar player worth a damn,' disapproving father Vernon Presley told his young son Elvis in 1954.

'This one I'm not letting out of my sight,' Joan Collins told a magazine interviewer in 1964 as she clung on to her new beau – Warren Beatty.

Hoorah for Hollywood, for all its falsity.

It'll never be possible to synchronise the voice with the pictures.
Movie mogul D. W. Griffiths, ruling
out the talkies

You're not the acting type.
Headmaster of Pembroke Lodge
School to one Alec Guinness.

In my opinion, she's nix.
Howard Hughes on Jean Harlow

Try another profession. Any other.
Head Instructor at John Murray
Anderson Drama School to Lucille
Ball

Never will Betty Bacall attain a caviar and champagne income.
Walter Thornton, model agency boss

Rock and Roll is phoney and false. And it's sung written and played for the most part by cretinous goons.

Frank Sinatra, 1957

I tell you flat, Elvis can't last.

Jackie Gleason, 1956

I have a responsibility to show that a young married couple can still be happy in our business.

Sonny Bono, of Sonny and Cher, 1965. They later split up

The Beatles? They're on the wane.

Prince Philip, 1965

I see on TV that Mick Jagger's copying my pouting bit. But I don't think it will work with him because when he pouts he looks like a basset hound.

P. J. Proby

Mick proposed to me last December. He was really nice about it. He got down on one knee. We'll be getting married next month.

Jerry Hall, October 1983

I don't believe in the institution of marriage any longer. It doesn't suit me. If other people want to go out and get married – wonderful. However, it won't be for me again.

Lesley Anne Down, March 1982. She wed film director Bill Friedkin four months later

Whatever anyone says, I'm the one he comes home to, aren't I?

Dee Harrington on Rod Stewart, March 1975, the month he met Britt Ekland

Press Howlers

Some newspapers are quick enough to set the world to rights. But they are just as prone to dropping bricks as the rest of us. Sometimes more so.

The *Sunday Express* overstepped itself with a campaign of overstatement about the up-and-coming Labour star Neil Kinnock. Three years before his election as leader, in July 1980, an article in the Crossbencher column said: 'Suddenly the belief that nothing could prevent him reaching the top has gone. And he is left instead with the uneasy thought "Have I gone and wrecked my chances when I have barely begun." '

A year later, Crossbencher was still trying to belittle 'that carrot-thatched chap from Bedwelty'. In November 1981, writing of the 'end of his hopes' they said: 'Suddenly he sees all his hopes crumbling away. And like the little boy watching the incoming tide destroy his sand-castle, there is nothing he can do about it.'

Mind you, the *Sunday Express* does not reach a worldwide audience. Imagine the red faces at the Reuters news agency in 1982 who ascribed the most undiplomatic of gaffes to Her Majesty the Queen. According to its teleprinter, talking of global recession during her visit to Los Angeles, the Queen said: 'Even this most vibrant of colonies has not been totally immune to the effects of the recession.'

Fortunately the error was corrected in time to prevent a rematch of the Wars of Independence. The agency's New York headquarters issued a hasty correction: 'For *colonies* read *economies*.'

Newspapers have had an unfortunate habit of tempting fate since time immemorial. In 1889 the *Literary Digest* declared: 'The horseless carriage is a luxury for the wealthy. It will never, of course, come into such common use as the bicycle.

While in 1902 *Harper's Weekly* opined: 'The actual building of roads devoted to motor cars is not for the near future, in spite of the many rumours to that effect.'

During his Presidency, Woodrow Wilson was the unfortunate victim of an even more unfortunate misprint. Reporting on his outing to the theatre, a correspondent wrote: 'Mr Wilson spent most of his time entertaining Mrs Galt.'

It appeared: 'Mr Wilson spent most of his time entering Mrs Galt.'

Even leading American columnist James Reston fell into the trap when he declared, in September 1964: H. S. Truman gave them hell in 1948, but LBJ has turned it round – he's giving them heaven.

But not for long, as it turned out.

In Britain *The Guardian* (hence its nickname *The Grauniad*) is noted for its bloomers. When Mr John Whitney was appointed head of the Independent Broadcasting Authority in April 1982, the paper's TV expert wrote: 'He is 61. His appointment only four years before his retirement age appears to be . . . a decision to go for a short term appointment.'

They should perhaps have bothered to check his age. Mr Whitney was, in fact, 51, which gave him a rather longer 14 years in which to make his mark.

Only slightly behind *The Guardian* in the clanger stakes is the London *Times*. In October 1983, the paper managed to carry a full obituary on racehorse owner Captain Marcos Lemos, one of the Turf's most colourful characters. As phone calls of condolence poured in to his home he had the rather unique privilege of being able to read his own obituary while walking round the saleroom of Newmarket bloodstock sales. Said Lemos, 56: 'I wondered why people were staring at me.'

Magazines too, can put their foot in it . . . all the more so when they are printed weeks in advance. The issue of *Mother and Baby* for March 1984 had a front page blurb on 'SECOND BABY – *Why even a Princess may have to wait*'. Inside, the main feature tried to explain why the Princess of Wales had not become pregnant. It was either the effects of dramatic weight loss or the stress of trying too hard, opined writer Theresa Graham.

Princess Diana's pregnancy was announced just as the magazine hit the streets – on 13 February 1984.

One of the most unhappy own goals to befall the newspaper world came the unlucky way of the *Daily Mail* in 1982 when thousands of readers simultaneously thought they had won the £35 000 jackpot in the newspaper's 'Casino' contest (an upmarket version of bingo). Cock-a-hoop would-be winners, some of them travelling hundreds of miles by taxi, some having abandoned expensive holidays to claim their winnings, descended on the newspaper's offices just off Fleet Street only to find a queue of several hundred would-be jackpot claimants. The 'winning' number had been shared by thousands.

The Western press is not the only culprit. In July 1983, Western media-spies spotted this Russian own goal.

A picture of commandos patrolling the Central American bush was captioned in the Moscow weekly journal *New Times* as 'Nicaraguan border guards constantly on combat preparedness against US-backed counter-revolutionaries.'

The next day the Soviet Army newspaper *Red Star* came out with the same photograph. This time, however, it was captioned: 'US-armed Nicaraguan counter-revolutionaries who have returned to their native land with the sole aim of overthrowing its lawful government.'

This desire to have things both ways is occasionally laid bare in the British press. In Cup Final week in May 1983, pouting nude model Corinne Russell was the well-endowed pin-up in both *The Sun* and the *Daily Star*. *The Sun* said she supported Brighton and Hove Albion. The *Daily Star* insisted she was a Manchester United fan.

A third newspaper decided to settle the argument. When interviewed she said: 'I'm not the least bit interested in football.'

In 1920 the *New York Times* poured scorn on a claim by leading space scientist Professor Robert Goddard that rockets could function in a vacuum, saying: 'He seems only to lack the knowledge ladled out daily in high schools.' When, forty-nine years later, in July 1969, the Apollo 11 probe proved Goddard right beyond any doubt, the *NY Times* published a correction: 'It is now definitely established that a rocket can function in a vacuum. *The Times* regrets its error.'

Some other notable acts of grovelling:

DIANA AND THE MIRROR: The *Daily Mirror* published a story on Page One on Saturday about the Princess of Wales visiting a little old lady in London.

A picture showed the Princess and her detective leaving an address in west London. Princess Diana was quoted as saying: 'I have been to see an old lady friend.'

In fact, the Princess was attending a private dance lesson. The *Daily Mirror* apologises for the error.

14 November 1983

CORRECTION: In the summary column the cryptic reference to a deceased Venezuelan President meeting great apes should have referred to President Betancur of Colombia meeting guerrillas.

Latin American Weekly Report,
November 1983

CORRECTION: In a report last week of the court case involving Mr . . . . . . of Dagenham, we wrongly stated that Mr . . . . . . had previously been found guilty of buggery. The charge referred to was, in fact, one of burglary.

Dagenham Post

THE LOUTH LEADER: Unfortunately our reporter misheard Mr . . . . . .'s solicitor, who did in fact say his 'present' girlfriend and not 'pregnant' as we inadvertently printed.

January 1983

CORRECTION: Due to a misunderstanding over the telephone we stated that the couple would live at the home of the bridegroom's father. We have been asked to point out that they will in fact live at the Old Manse.

English newspaper, quoted by Fritz
Spiegl in 'The Black on White
Misprint Show.'

Paper Talk

'Foreign Secretary Francis Pym will become Home Secretary in a major cabinet shuffle following a Tory election victory,' said Walter Terry of *The Sun* in June 1983.

Oh dear. He was despatched, instead, to the back benches.

ALL SAVED FROM TITANIC AFTER COLLISION' reported the *Evening Star*, New York, on 15 April 1912.

The pressures of trying to be authoritative, and trying to be first with a story, do sometimes lead to the odd error.

MIRROR EXCLUSIVE:
KOO TO MEET ANDREW AT BALMORAL
Prince Andrew and Koo Stark are bound for a secret rendezvous at Balmoral Castle, the Queen's Scottish home.

They will meet up at the end of next week after the Prince arrives back in Britain from a holiday in Canada.

. . . Her visit will be seen by many as a 'reward' for her faultless public behaviour.

Daily Mirror, *2 August 1983.*
Needless to say, it didn't happen. Koo
went to Australia instead.

Still, the facts didn't deter *The Sun* the next day:
KOO'S ROYAL APPOINTMENT
REWARD FOR A GIRL WHO DID NOT TELL
Prince Andrew's gorgeous girlfriend Koo Stark has been given the Royal seal of approval. Koo's personal invitation to spend her summer holidays with the Queen at Balmoral Castle in a fortnight's time was by Royal appointment.

The Queen herself wrote in Koo's name among the group of guests invited to the romantic Scottish castle.

The Sun, *3 August 1983. Oh dear,*
they made it up again.

There must be now a reasonable chance that the SDP alliance will win the next general election outright.

Malcolm Rutherford, political editor,
Financial Times, *February 1982*

YES, A SECOND LITTLE WALES *IS* ON THE WAY
It seems likely that Prince Charles will use the occasion of his 35th birthday on November 14 to announce that the Princess of Wales is expecting a second child.

Over the past few months ill-informed reports in Fleet Street have claimed, then been forced to retract, that the Princess was pregnant. However, I am able to confirm that the Royal couple are now happily expecting a spring 1984 baby.

> Daily Express, *October 1983. They*
> *had to retract. She* did *become*
> *pregnant – but not until Christmas.*

Amid a series of agonised Aarghs! from actors approached for the role, I can reveal that the search for a screen Superman is at last over. He is Nick Nolte, 35 year old son of a salesman, who has been chosen for the role after refusals from Robert Redford, Steve McQueen, James Caan and Paul Newman.

> Daily Mail *diary, October 1976. But*
> *what of Christopher Reeve?*

I have it on the greatest authority that the next General Election will not take place before 1984 . . . and remember that you read it here first!

> *Nigel Dempster*, Daily Mail, *January*
> *1983. We remember. The election*
> *took place in June 1983*

Finally, to those *doubles entendres* we have all come to know and love:

UNPRECEDENTED EVENT – UNDERGRADUATES
SCRATCH BALLS
Famous Oxford Mail *headline*

MAN CRITICAL AFTER BUS BACKS INTO HIM
Middleton Press. *Well, he would be,*
wouldn't he?

Watch our for the free supplement in next month's issue:
BRIDES' FIRST COCKERY COURSE.

Women's magazine, quoted by Fritz
Spiegl

YOU KNOW WHERE YOU CAN PUT IT!

Headline in *Woman*

Yes, Madam – I do indeed.

The World's Most Disaster-Prone Politician

James Watt, US Secretary for Agriculture under Ronald
Reagan, holds the record for the most super-bloops in the
political world.

He starred in a 30-month whirlwind career of boner, insult,
and invective before his tongue finally got the better of him in
October 1983, and he was forced to resign.

It was estimated that during his short spell in office, Watt had
managed to offend 85 per cent of the population of America.

He upset environmentalists by likening them to Communists
and the Nazi party in Germany 'in their pursuit of centralised
planning and control of the economy'.

He upset Democrats by telling Californian farmers in 1981 'I
never use the words Democrats and Republicans. It's Liberals
and Americans.'

He upset women's groups by comparing abortion supporters
with 'the forces which shaped the holocaust'.

He upset pop (and even light music) fans by banning The
Beach Boys from the 1983 July 4 celebration in Washington,
saying rock music was 'unfit for patriotic Americans'.

That rankled with the Reagan camp because Vice-President
Bush had worked hard to get the Californian group to endorse
the Reagan campaign of 1980. Watt was forced to grovel
publicly to the President and emerge humbled from the Oval
Office clutching a special presentation – a plaster cast of a foot
with a bullet hole in it.

Watt also:
- Attracted a 6 million dollar lawsuit after getting fired an oil lobbyist who wrote to him asking for an explanation of his 'liberals and Americans' jibe.
- Was forced to apologise after saying an opponent was 'probably a registered left-winger'. He turned out to be a registered Republican.
- Caused a diplomatic storm by writing to the Israeli Ambassador warning US support for Israel could be curbed if Jewish liberals opposed his hard-line energy programme.
- Had to apologise to American Indians after calling their reservations 'shameful examples of the failure of socialism', with the highest rates in the country for unemployment, drug and alcohol abuse, and VD.

Finally, Watt brought his relentless own goal-scoring of the previous two and a half years to a majestic climax in September 1983, when he said of members of his newly-appointed Coal Lease Commission: 'We have every kind of mix you can have. A black, a woman, two Jews, and a cripple.'

Congressman Tom Downey of New York extended Watt 'The Earl Butz Racial and Religious Sensitivity Award' (in honour of the US Agriculture Secretary who resigned in 1976 after derogatory remarks against blacks), while Rep. Joseph Markley of Massachusetts said: 'James Watt has done what Don Rickles in his best skit could never do – offend nearly our entire population in one sentence.'

Cartoonist Englehart drew out Watt's Coal Lease Commission members. A black, a woman, two Jews . . . and a man who had just shot himself through both feet. The 'cripple' was James Watt. His resignation followed soon afterwards – the end of an incredible public career.

9

Thank Goodness it's Only a Game . . .

Sporting Losers

American golfer Doug Sanders isn't remembered for machine-like performances. Indeed, the most famous moment for the 'Playboy of the Golf World' came when he scored an incredible golfing own goal.

Sanders had just to sink a two-and-a-half foot putt on the 18th green to win the 1970 British Open at St Andrews. Unbelievably he fluffed it – 'my mind wandered to how some people throw the ball or putter into the air when they win' – then went on to lose in the play-off to the more steely nerved Jack Nicklaus.

There was Don Fox, the Wakefield Trinity goal kicker whose 'miss of the century' at Wembley in May 1968, gave Leeds the Rugby League Challenge Cup by 11 points to 10. It should have been one of the simplest kicks of his career, but he sliced it wide. He said: 'It was the worst moment of my life. I just wanted to go home and die.'

There was the 17-year-old jockey Joey Brown who in the lead at Windsor racetrack in 1980, mistook the winning post, pulled up and let the rest of the riders past.

With its rich rewards and the knife-edge between victory and the ever yawning jaws of defeat, sport has produced some amazing examples of self-inflicted misery.

Fred Merkle, of the New York Giants, managed to lose a crucial game in 1908 by running for the clubhouse too soon. Seeing a team-mate hit the winning run in the needle match with Chicago Cubs, Merkle didn't bother to complete his journey from first base to second. Instead he sprinted to the clubhouse as the crowd invaded the field. But an opponent picked up the ball, touched second, and called him out. The game was abandoned as a tie and later replayed. Merkle's Giants lost.

The annual Oxford v Cambridge boat race has brought some memorable scenes. Cambridge sank in 1857 and 1978; Oxford in 1925 and 1951. But in 1912 BOTH crews found themselves in the murky waters of the Thames.

On March 29, with a gale blowing, the Cambridge crew went down swamped after seven minutes and had to swim ashore. All Oxford had to do was to complete the course. They sank four minutes later.

The Dark Blues managed to reach the bank, bail out their boat, and make it to Mortlake (with one hiccup: one of the crew spotted a friend and made off into the crowd. It took some minutes to find the absent oarsman and get started again). But, unfortunately, it was decided Oxford had been helped by spectators and 'no race' was called.

Oxford won the re-race after both crews suffered the humiliation of using 'water wings'. Huge inflatable bladders were attached to the boats to make sure they did not sink.

Yet even the 1912 crews could not rival the own goal of Cambridge cox Peter Hobson who, in 1984, managed to write off their £7000 boat before they had even reached the starting line.

Hobson failed to see a tethered barge and the boat slammed straight into it before jack-knifing and breaking in two, to the surprise, consternation, and resultant soaking of his crew.

The BBC scored their own 'first'. Having spent many thousands of pounds on TV coverage of every inch of the course, including hiring a helicopter to fly overhead, their cameras managed to miss completely the historic and glorious moment of impact.

But the real shame was Hobson's. Afterwards it was revealed it was not his first encounter with a large stationary object. Supremely tempting fate, he had listed his hobby in the boat race programme as 'reshaping barges'.

The Turf has also been known to hear the cry of 'No Race'. In September 1972, the Loadman Novices' Chase at Hexham was declared void after the two runners managed 22 refusals between them.

The horses in one of the most farcical races of all time were Ann Rose, and the inappropriately named Fearless Footsteps. Both approached the first at little more than a walk. They both refused the sixth and seventh, but carried on at the second attempt. Fearless Footsteps refused the eighth and Ann Rose the ninth.

A second attempt got the filly safely over but at the tenth, she unseated her rider, Ronald Smedley. Three more attempts ended in failure and Smedley decided to give up.

Meanwhile, seeing his chance of glory if only he could get the horse round the course, rider Barry Sayles had no fewer than 12 tries at the eighth before he decided Fearless Footsteps wasn't all that fearless after all and returned shamefaced to the paddock.

American football doesn't quite have the instant own goals of soccer, but there have been occasions when pro-ball players have tried their best to hit the self-flagellation hall of fame.

In 1929 Roy Riegles, side lineman for the University of California, managed to pick up a loose ball with the score 7–6 and sprint most of the field to his end zone for a two-point safety, when he thought he was on his way to a touchdown. It gave his opponents, Georgia Tech, the national collegiate championship.

He said later he'd heard the crowd all shouting furiously but thought they were cheering him on.

In October 1964, defensive end Jim Marshall of the Minnesota Vikings repeated Riegles' feat with a 50 ft dash to his end zone. He didn't feel quite as bad, though, as his team still won.

From the most American of games to the most English. In July 1974, Indian batsman Ashok Mankad managed to dismiss himself – with his cap.

As Mankad was trying to fend away a short-pitched delivery from Chris Old in the Edgbaston Test, the ball spun off his glove, flicked the peak of his cap, and was knocked backwards onto the stumps.

Said Mankad, who was on 43 and looked set for a big innings: 'It might have missed the wicket, but the wind caught it and blew it back, and off came the bails.'

The unfortunate batsman – who continued to wear his cap afterwards – was given out hit-wicket.

Young matador, Francisco Espia, 21, virtually ruined his career in 1983 when he became only the second matador in Spanish history to be found drunk in charge of his sword, and thrown out of the ring.

Locals were staggered when Espia, who fought under the title 'The Gypsy' turned up in their bar in Seville just before what was to be the most important fight of his career. He had one brandy to steady his nerves . . . then another . . . and another . . . and another.

When' he finally made it into the arena it became clear that 'The Gypsy' was somewhat tipsy. He astonished the crowd by removing his shoes, before standing in the centre of the ring, limply holding his red cape and swaying.

Officials ordered him taken out of the ring and breathalysed. The test showed him well over the limit for driving, let alone bullfighting, and he was sent home in disgrace.

A 'knock-out' cricket cup in Sheffield, Yorkshire, in June 1983, turned out to be just that when two batsmen collided head on going for a quick run.

Opening bats Paul Webb, 31, and Chris George, 33, of the Midland Bank side knocked themselves right out of the game with a local works side.

Paul, of Chesterfield, had to be stretchered off and spent 36 hours in hospital. Chris, of Sheffield, needed 16 stitches in a gash on his chin. He said: 'It was a chance in a million.'

Needless to say the Midland Bank team progressed no further in the knock-out cup. They were knocked out by six wickets.

While talking of the more violent side of sport, just before the 1984 Super Bowl, Pete Cronon, 17-stone linebacker with the hot favourites, the Washington Redskins, had this to say about one of his Los Angeles Raiders opponents:

'Destroying him is like killing a fly. I'd catch that fly. I'd shake it up in that bare hand. When he got dizzy, I'd let him down. Then I'd rip his wings off, let him crawl around and suffer for an hour or so.

'And when I knew I couldn't miss, I'd take an axe to him.'

Nice to know that bad guys don't always come first:

Cronon's team, defying all the experts and every prediction, were humiliated. 'Punching themselves on the nose and tripping over their own feet,' as one writer called it, they surrendered to the Raiders 38–9, the largest margin of defeat in the competition's history.

Finally, fast bowler Stan Webb of Plymouth club Breton was giving the opposing Torpoint side something to think about in the local league needle match in August 1971.

Until something happened which totally altered the course of the game. Lanky Stan came in on his long run-up . . . and his trousers came catapulting down. The poor pace bowler fell flat on his face.

The batsman shouldn't have laughed. When the 6ft 4in budding Brian Rix had girded his loins again, he managed to bowl him clean out next ball.

Though at the end of the over, and with his trousers once again making for his ankles, the partly-clad paceman had no extra cover, and made for home.

Said a saddened Stan: 'It was an awful let-down. If only my trousers had stayed up, I'm sure we would have won.'

Have you ever heard a better line from a loser than that?

He'll Fall in Six

'You're next, big mouth,' Sonny Liston foolishly said to Cassius Clay after beating Floyd Patterson in 1963.

'Burnley will be the team of the seventies,' said an optimistic Jimmy Adamson in 1971. They weren't.

'I intend to make the West Indies grovel' said Tony Grieg in 1976 before they came and whipped England 3–0, the team's worst drubbing on their own soil since defeat by Bradman's Australians in 1948.

Sport does tend to bring out the blarney in people.

> Watching an America's Cup race is like watching grass grow.
>
> *Ring Lardner. Try telling that to an*
> *Australian*

> Lawn tennis, though an excellent game in every respect is, nevertheless, one in which middle aged people, especially ladies, cannot engage in with satisfaction to themselves, and its rapidly waning popularity is largely due to this fact.
> *The Isthmian Book of Croquet, 1899*

> ITALY LIKELY TO REGAIN WORLD CUP
> *Unpatriotic headline in* The Times
> *which might have been all right in*
> *1982 . . . but not July 1966, when*
> *England won!*

> Frazier will fall in six.
> *Muhammed Ali, for once on his way*
> *to defeat, March 1981*

> Overall fair, but would improve if he paid more attention to his studies and less to the game of golf. It is not a team sport and holds no future for him.
> *School report on leading British golfer*
> *Peter Alliss*

Girls don't play cricket.
> *Unfriendly policeman stopping*
> *8-year-old Rachel Heyhoe practising*
> *in the street*

Cassius Clay is gone forever. There is no way he can recapture the past or return to his prime.
> *Gene Ward, sports editor,* Chicago
> Tribune, *1970. But he did.*

We'll get out of trouble.
> *Jimmy Melia, manager of Brighton,*
> *April 1983, before they lost the FA*
> *Cup Final, were relegated and he was*
> *sacked.*

She won't win a game.
> *Fred Perry on the clash of Billie-Jean*
> *King and Bobby Riggs, 1973. She*
> *won handsomely.*

Tunes of glory will vibrate round the world for Britain's Tony Sibson tonight. Like so many others who have recently fallen under Sibson's spell, I see him pounding his way to a titanic British triumph.
> *Peter Batt,* Daily Star, *February 1983.*
> *Sibson lost.*

Soccer Own Goals

If soccer is the stage for the most spectacular own goals, one man will go down as a legend in the art – Leeds United goalkeeper Gary Sprake.

Sprake's five star blunder in Leeds United's top of the table clash with Liverpool in December 1967, brought the goal of a lifetime. After 44 minutes, Liverpool were winning 1–0. Sprake gathered the ball, made to throw it to one of his players . . . but didn't let go.

The ball curled straight into his own net with the hapless goalkeeper looking helplessly on.

Liverpool's famous 'Kop' immediately broke into a rendering of the Des O'Connor hit 'Careless Hands'.

Said Sprake: 'I thought we were coming back into the game at the time. I was going to throw the ball out to one of our players but changed my mind and went to pull it into my body. It slipped and went in.'

The Leeds United man never recovered from his 'butter-fingers' reputation, letting the ball bounce off his legs to Martin Chivers to help Tottenham win 1–0 18 months later, and, on being transferred to Birmingham, almost immediately conceding an own goal to Everton. He said of this one: 'I thought it was going to be a centre, but it turned out to be a shot.' Said Everton forward John Connolly: 'I've got news for you, it was meant to be a centre.'

'Mad Albert' Iremonger, the goalie for Notts County, was 6ft 6in tall and his clowning antics were a favourite with the Nottingham crowd. But once, when he stepped up to take a penalty for his club against Sheffield Wednesday in 1925, he realised he had gone a little too far.

'Mad Albert's' powerful shot struck the Wednesday crossbar, and rebounded down the pitch. There followed a frantic Keystone Cops chase as Wednesday tried to drive the ball into the unguarded net before Iremonger got back into position.

A Wednesday player punted the ball into the County goal-mouth but Albert refused to give up the chase. He managed to draw level with the ball at about the penalty spot and took an almighty swipe to clear it.

You guessed. He looked on, panting and disbelieving, as the ball screamed into the roof of his own net.

Rivelino of Brazil holds the record for the quickest goal ever scored . . . after just three seconds. But it was something of an own goal by the goalkeeper in the Brazilian League match in 1974, though he never touched the ball.

For the goalie was *on his knees praying* as the match kicked off. Rivelino saw him looking skyward and hammered home a shot from 55 yards.

The goalkeeper feared even worse when a spectator ran on to the field waving a pistol. Murder was averted, however, when the angry fan fired six shots into the ball before escaping back into the crowd.

The fastest own goal in a major match came from former England wing half Alan Mullery, playing for Fulham against Sheffield Wednesday in 1961. He managed to put the ball past his own goalkeeper in 20 seconds without a Wednesday player so much as touching the ball.

'I shall never forget it,' lamented Mullery later. 'Almost from the kick-off I received the ball just outside our area. I decided to pass back. By the time I realised our keeper was out of his goal, I had hit the ball – and it rolled over the line.' It was the start of a drubbing for Fulham, who lost 6–1.

On 29 April 1972, Millwall fans celebrated their promotion to the First Division. Crowds surged onto the pitch to chair their heroes off the field after a 2–0 win over Preston in the last game of the season. Players had their shirts ripped off their backs, the loudspeakers blared out 'Congratulations', and the directors ordered champagne.

News had been flashed to the ground that Millwall's promotion rivals Birmingham had lost 2–1 to Sheffield Wednesday. But it was a sad case of counting chickens . . . Birmingham had *won* 2–1. They were going up – not Millwall.

Finally a brave journalist took the correct result up to the Club's broadcasting box, and the revelry turned to anger. Said manager Benny Fenton: 'It was most upsetting.'

Those on the touchlines have been known to score the odd own goal themselves. Morton 'A' team manager Jim Devlin thought his team were lacking somewhere but couldn't work out what. It just didn't add up. At half time he realised . . . he had only sent out ten men.

One of soccer's greatest boobs was not made either by a player or a manager . . . it was made by the club secretary. Birmingham City forgot to send their forms back in 1928 for entry into the FA Cup. They were barred from the competition – the only senior club to crash out of the competition by administrative error.

Colchester goalkeeper Graham Smith went through his usual pre-match routine. He kicked first the foot of one post, then he jogged across the goal and kicked the foot of the other. Then the crossbar fell on his head.

Port Vale defenders couldn't understand why their goalkeeper was grovelling on the ground after Sheffield United had scored in a Second Division match in December 1892. They moved to help him, but there was a sickening crunch – and all was revealed. The goalkeeper had been trying to find his glasses, which had come off when the goal was scored. The 'helpful' defender had just trodden on them.

Unsurprisingly, Port Vale went on to make something of a spectacle of themselves, losing by a massive ten goals to nil.

His colleagues told the goalkeeper not to argue with the centre forward about his goal. And they were right. A few seconds later the angry striker shot him dead.

The ultimate penalty was paid by goalkeeper Amador Madero in an amateur match in Mexico City in January 1974. After they rowed, striker Eusebio Rosas rushed to the touchline, produced a pistol, and riddled the poor goalkeeper with bullets. He died instantly.

Finally, the too-eager substitute. Dick Long couldn't wait to get on to the pitch to play for his works team at Aylesbury, Bucks, in October 1979. He tore off his track suit and dashed on to the field . . . then, to shrieks from the crowd, rushed back off again. He had forgotten to put on his shorts.

12 Top Gaffes from the Sports Commentary Box

1　The band playing, the tents with their club flags, the famous lime tree, people picnicking round the ground, whilst on the field hundreds of small boys are playing with their balls.

*Rex Alston, BBC cricket
commentator, describing the scene at
Canterbury*

2　He's pulling out the big one. He's whacking in the big one. If she hits the board and bags a big one, that'll put her in the bronze medal position.

*Ron Pickering, BBC athletics
commentator*

3 Henry Horton's got a funny sort of stance. It looks as if he's shitting on a sooting stick.

Brian Johnston, BBC cricket
commentator

4 He has had seven craps as scrum half for England.

Linkman Jimmy Hill handing over to
rugby commentator Nigel
Starmer-Smith

5 If there's a pileup there, they'll have to give some of the players artificial insemination.

Curt Cowdy, US Profootball
commentator

6 Torocsik got impatient and simply decided to have a slash.

Soccer summariser Ron Greenwood
on the sending off of Hungary's centre
forward in the 1978 World Cup

7 The girls in front are breaking wind.

Anonymous US commentator on
women's cycling event at the 1984
Los Angeles Olympics

8 She's fully exposed herself at the front.

Athletics summariser Brendan Foster
on women's marathon gold medallist
Joan Benoit, also at Los Angeles

9 There was a chink in Zhu's armour.

Los Angeles foot-in-mouth gold
medallist David Coleman, discussing
the failure of – you guessed – the
Chinese world high jump champion,
Zhu Jian Hua

10 Bad luck on Peter. He's obviously in great pain and has probably broken his ankle. It's especially bad luck as he is here on his honeymoon with his pretty young wife. Still,

he'll probably be all right tomorrow, if he sticks it up tonight.

Brian Johnston at the Scarborough
cricket festival on an injury to South
African Peter Pollock

11 His tail is literally up.

Trevor Bailey, BBC cricket
commentator

12 This is Cunis at the Vauxhall End, Cunis – a funny sort of name. Neither one thing nor the other.

Alan Gibson (attrib.) at the Oval test
with New Zealand, 1969

22 *Doubles Entendres* Specifically to be Avoided in Polite Company

Certain words – and phrases – are a sure way to score an embarrassing social own goal. Here is Jones's early warning list of the danger words and how they can be turned so easily into embarrassing gaffes.

Nothing on	e.g., I'd be delighted to come, I've got nothing on.
At it	e.g., They were at it all afternoon.
Put it	e.g., He's just looking for somewhere to put it.
Up and down	e.g., The two of them have been up and down all day.
Under	e.g., She is under him at work.
Club	e.g., She's in the club too now.
Come	e.g., She thought he was never coming.
Position	e.g., What do you think of the Nicaraguan position?
Nibble	e.g., I don't want a proper meal, but I'll come round for a quick nibble.
Milkman	e.g., She's been waiting in all day for the milkman.

Organ	e.g., He's got a very large private organ.
Bed	e.g., She's in bed with something she picked up on the bus home.
Erection	e.g., What a hideous erection. How long has it been up?
Play	e.g., He's been playing with it all afternoon.
Feel	e.g., He hasn't been feeling himself recently.
Relief	e.g., He found a good way to relieve himself.
Member	e.g., Some of the members have been looking a bit peaky recently.
Bottom	e.g., At bottom, he was always ready to accommodate.
Seat	e.g., In the Liberal Party, there are hardly any safe seats.
Tool	e.g., What a useful looking tool.
Ball	e.g., The regiment has the best ceremonial balls.
Faggots, Rissoles	e.g., He's become very partial to faggots. And rissoles too.

10

Let's not Forget the Ultimate Own Goal

Meeting One's Maker

Own goals are a common, if unfortunate way, of falling victim to the grim reaper. Thousands each year meet their maker at their own hands when everyday situations go terribly wrong.

An Italian wife was found shot through the heart on a bed in Naples. The bullet had come from a gun lying on the bedside table.

Murder? Suicide? No. Incredibly, forensic tests showed the woman had been shot dead by a moth in an incredible act of revenge. The insect had flown into the flame of her bedside candle and been frazzled to death. Its body had plummeted down on to the hair trigger of the gun and it had fired.

A Manchester man was killed by a lawn mower. The blades struck a live cartridge which had been discarded in the grass. The bullet went off and lodged in the poor man's brain.

German artist Daniel Hager was killed by one of his own sculptures. While he was putting the final touches to a work that had taken him years to make, his chisel lopped off a four-inch sharpened sliver of marble. The sliver pierced poor Herr Hager to the heart, killing him instantly.

Invention has been the mother of some cruel twists of fate. In the 1760s, Professor Richman of St Petersburg joined the race to be the first to invent the lightning conductor. He fried.

A warning for 'Hurricane' Higgins. In Melbourne, Australia, a man died from an over-enthusiastic snooker shot. He had been happily potting in his garage with a friend when he decided to show off a trick shot. Clambering on to a beam in the ceiling and suspending himself by his feet, he then attempted the shot of a lifetime. It turned out that way, too. He fell head first on to the concrete floor and died soon afterwards from brain damage.

There are some who one can't help feeling tempted providence just a little too much.

One of New Zealand's most outspoken critics of capital punishment was one D. H. Beenan. In 1976 he staged a special demonstration of how barbaric hanging was. Standing on a chair and slipping a noose around his neck, he told his audience 'how horrible the whole thing is'. He then parted company from the chair and broke his neck.

The aptly-named Charles Justice, an inmate at Ohio State Penitentiary, was a valued soul there and in 1897 helped design the jail's first electric chair. You guessed . . . after being released he was convicted of murder, and was awarded the ultimate honour of testing his own workmanship.

Another case of a famous person becoming a victim of their work came with the death of super-illusionist Harry Houdini. One of Houdini's tricks was to hold his stomach muscles rigid and ask people to rain blows on his midriff which, he claimed, was impervious to pain.

What he hadn't reckoned on was a 'fan' trying this when he least expected it. In his dressing room in Montreal in 1926 Houdini was given a fierce blow by a student. His stomach muscles were relaxed and he took the full force of the punch. For once Houdini couldn't escape – he contracted peritonitis and died a few days later.

Richard Drasser, an American visitor to the tiny north Australian town of Babinda in October 1983, scoffed when he heard of the legend of 'The Devil's Hole'. The pond near the town was said to have claimed fourteen victims after an aborigine curse.

Legend had it that a 17-year-old aborigine girl, Oolana, was married to Dyga, 18. Both were members of the Edinji tribe, but Oolana fell in love with Waronoo, a handsome young man from another tribe, and they ran away together.

Angry Edinjis then chased and caught the couple near the Devil's Hole. They killed Waroonoo before the girl's eyes, whereupon she threw herself into the water and drowned.

Drasser, 25, laughed at the notice which read 'These waters are dangerous', and stripped off for a swim. After a few strokes he slipped beneath the waters and disappeared.

He had become the fifteenth victim of the Devil's Hole.

Movie newcomer Mark Frechette was the male lead in Michelangelo Antonioni's 1970 film, *Zabriskie Point*. In it he played a disaffected youth who turned to crime, and eventually died in police custody. In real life, in April 1974, disaffected Frechette, who had joined a commune, was jailed in Boston for six to fifteen years for attempted robbery. In September 1975, in custody in Norfolk, Mass., he was found dead, a 150 lb weight-lifting bar having allegedly fallen on his throat.

A top £1000-a-week striker with an Italian first division soccer club got himself shot dead in a jape in a jeweller's shop that badly backfired. Italian international Luciano Re Cecconi, 28, walked into the shop in Rome with two friends in January, 1977, and joked: 'Hands up, this is a robbery.'

Unfortunately the jeweller not only took him seriously, but beneath the counter he had a loaded gun ready for just such an emergency. He pulled out the pistol and shot Luciano dead with a single bullet.

Said the jeweller afterwards: 'I'm not a soccer fan.'

Famous Last Words

'This *noblesse* will ruin us,' said Marie Antoinette – correctly as it turned out.

'There's nothing about my life that is an accident,' said Marc Bolan shortly before dying in a car crash.

'People like their blues singers dead,' opined Janis Joplin.

Some verbal own goals by the departed will always stay with us:

> Who could imagine that life would be so sad, I wish I could die.
>> *Vincent Van Gogh, after shooting himself at the home of his doctor, July 1890. He then did.*

> I have promised the Prime Minister I will be back in London by October 20.
>> *Lord Thomson, Air Minister, before boarding the doomed R101 airship, October 1930*

> I believe the only way to reform people is to kill them.
>> *Car Panzram, US mass murderer, hanged at Fort Leavenworth, September 1930*

> I've never felt better.
>> *Douglas Fairbanks, dying words*

> My fun days are over.
>> *James Dean, shortly before his fatal car crash*

> What is perfect? Perfect is death. It's a physical death. Termination.
>> *Jimi Hendrix*

> I will not resign. I declare my will to resist by every means, even at the cost of my life.
>> *Salvador Allende, September 1973. It cost him his life*

> I still believe I have a mission to carry out to the end, and I intend to carry it out to the end without giving up my throne . . . I'm convinced the monarchy in Iran will last longer than your regimes . . .
>> *Shah of Iran, October 1973*

I don't care what they say. Jimmy Hoffa can take care of himself.

Jimmy Hoffa, notorious leader of the
US teamsters' union, who
'disappeared' in 1975

I hate to say it, but crime is an overhead you have to pay if you want to live in this city.

George Moscone, Mayor of San
Francisco, December 1976. Shortly
afterwards he was shot dead by a
disgruntled constituent

When I left England, I still couldn't go on the street . . . it took me years to unwind. I would be walking round tense like, waiting for somebody to say something or jump me. I can go right out of this door now and go in a restaurant. You want to know how great that is?

John Lennon, on living in New York,
1980

12 Five-Star Suicides

1   SMALL SCREEN SUICIDE

Twenty-nine-year-old Miss Christine Chubbock, a newsreader for Miami's WXLT-TV entered the own-goal hall of fame by shooting herself dead on the air in July 1974. Facing the cameras, she coolly stated: 'In keeping with Channel 40's policy of bringing you the latest in blood and guts, you're going to see a first, an attempted suicide.' A perfectionist to the end, she had even written her demise into her copy of the script.

2   PEACE AT LAST

Roy Cleveland, 71, created a world record by being struck by lightning seven times and surviving each time. He was apparently none too happy about it. In September 1983, at Waynesboro, Virginia, he shot himself to death.

3   SIXTH TIME LUCKY

Lovesick Hans Finer of Klagenfurt, Austria, found in 1967 that it isn't all that easy to end it all. His plan was to steal a car and crash it into a tree. He ended up stealing four. The first car wasn't fast enough. The second broke down. He crashed the third – but walked out unhurt. When he stole a fourth vehicle, police arrested him. So he tried suicide a fifth time – by plunging a dagger into his chest. Surgeons saved his life. Finally after being sentened to two years for car thefts, Hans achieved his ambition. He jumped 30 feet through the courtroom windows . . . to his death.

4 THE VANISHING PREMIER

Australian Prime Minister, Harold Holt, 60, sparked off some bizarre rumours when he walked into a wild surf in December 1967 at Portsea, Victoria, and was never seen again. Among the most bizarre suggestions were assassination by the CIA and that he was a Red China spy and was on his way to be picked up in secret by a Chinese submarine. His almost certain rendezvous, however, was with that great I-spy in the sky.

5 HE JUMPED TOO SOON

Chip shop owner Herman Holt, 55, of Halifax, Australia, was worried about his income tax. Very worried in fact. A stern letter from the Inland Revenue convinced him he was about to be sent a massive tax demand and be ruined. So he threw himself under a train. Did Mr Holt ever find out? The taxman owed *him* $1400, not the other way round.

6 'IT'S NOT LOADED'

Rock musician Terry Kath, 33, singer with the group Chicago, got too friendly with a loaded automatic pistol at a friend's house in Los Angeles in January 1978. Pointing it at his temple, Russian roulette style, he told his friends: 'Don't worry, it's not loaded. See!' But the gun was loaded. Kath died instantly.

7 NOTHING LEFT TO CHANCE

Frenchman Jacques Lefèvre almost had to give up after what was planned as the most thorough of suicides. M. Lefèvre tied a noose around his neck, then fixed the other end to a stake at the top of a cliff. Just to make sure, he drank some poison, set his clothes alight, and, as he threw himself over the cliff, tried to shoot himself in the head. Regrettably the bullet cut the rope in two, he fell into the sea, where the salt water doused the flames and caused him to vomit the poison. He was picked up by a fisherman and taken to hospital, where he died of something he hadn't accounted for – exposure.

8   STRANGE DEATH OF SUPERMAN

Called to a house in Hollywood in October 1970, Los Angeles police unravelled the strange fantasy world of a 24-year-old man who neighbours wouldn't allow to play Superman. Arthur Mandelko, 24, was found dead inside a refrigerator held closed from the inside by a rope. It was revealed that every other night, Mandelko would don a Superman costume and go out into the city night, jumping from rooftop to rooftop. But his flying adventures had come to an abrupt end when other residents complained of the thumping sounds he made when leaping from roof to roof. He got round their objections by wearing his Superman kit under the uniform of a Los Angeles police patrolman. But the real police had put a stop to this, too, by cautioning him for using a red light and a siren on his motor cycle.

9   HE SLEEPS WITH THE FISHES

In July 1983, an unidentified man who believed he would be reincarnated as a fish threw himself into the river Seine and drowned. Police at Argenteuil, France, said they had found a letter explaining his beliefs in his jacket pocket.

10   OUT WITH A BANG

Seized by melancholy after his wife had left him, John Stratton decided to end it all by putting his head in a gas oven. He knelt down by the cooker and waited patiently for eternal sleep. He had forgotten, however, that his supply had recently been converted to natural gas, which is non-toxic. Pondering on his narrow escape, Mr Stratton decided to light a cigarette to celebrate. It was a bad decision. The room was by now full of gas, which if not poisonous is still extremely explosive. It blew the house sky high, Mr Stratton, second time lucky, included.

11   FOR SCIENCE . . .

In 1976, a 77-year-old man who was not identified, walked into the medical department of the University at Tallus, France, and announced: 'I wish to donate my body to science and I don't want to wait any longer.' He then took out a revolver and shot himself through the head. His gift was accepted.

12 GERONIMO!
A Yorkshire man told an inquest in 1983 how he had watched his brother climb 200 ft to the top of the transporter bridge which links Middlesborough and West Hartlepool, then, with a cry of 'Geronimo!' leap into the River Tees. His body was not recovered. The dead man's brother told the coroner: 'He was a happy-go-lucky sort of chap.'

Leading Own Goalscorers of America and Britain, and their Jones Own Goal Rating

AMERICA

1	JAMES WATT	(Supreme, consistent and uncompromising record of gaffes while in office)	9.8
2	GENERAL CUSTER	(The little big sacrifice)	9.7
3	THOMAS A. DEWEY	(Spectacular election defeats against all odds)	9.2
4	SPIRO T. AGNEW	(He really went for getting pole-axed as V-P)	9.2
5	JIMMY CARTER	(Defeated incumbent, nearly taken hostage by bunny rabbit)	8.4
6	WALTER MONDALE	(What can one say?)	8.3
7	EDWARD KENNEDY	(Would you go swimming with this man?)	8.2
8	GERALD FORD	(Uh?)	7.8
9	RICHARD NIXON	(Expletive deleted)	7.7

10	ED MUSKIE	(Shed a little tear)	7.5
11	HERBERT HOOVER	(Damn!)	7.2
12	JIM MORRISON	(Drug death pop star)	6.4
13	DAVID STOCKMAN	(This doesn't add up)	6.4
14	RONALD REAGAN	(Sometimes a hard act to swallow)	6.2
15	H. R. HALDEMAN	(He was only giving orders)	6.0
16	FRED MERKLE	(Giant among own goalscorers)	6.0
17	JANIS JOPLIN	(People like their blues singers . . .)	5.8
18	LIZA MINNELLI	(The bigger they ain't)	5.6
19	THE SECURITY GUARD WHO DISCOVERED THE WATERGATE BURGLARS AND IS THE ONLY MAN NOT TO HAVE BECOME RICH OUT OF THE WHOLE AFFAIR		5.2
20	JOHN GLENN	(He really came down to earth with a bump)	5.0

BRITAIN

1	NEVILLE CHAMBERLAIN	('I have here a piece of paper.')	9.7
2	MICHAEL FOOT	('Onward to victory.')	9.5
3	ANTHONY EDEN	(Suez)	9.2
4	LORD DACRE	(Whose reputation gradually dissolved . . .)	8.9
5	IAN SPROAT	(Caught carpetbagging)	8.8
6	P. J. PROBY	(All downhill since he split his trousers, and downhill on top of that)	8.7
7	EDWARD HEATH	(Ask a silly question)	8.6

8	CECIL PARKINSON	(A right man to choose)	8.5
9	SIMON DEE	(Who?)	8.3
10	JAMES CALLAGHAN	('Suntan? What suntan?')	7.4
11	PRINCE ANDREW	(For Vicki Hodge, and that School Dinners stunt)	7.3
12	BRIAN JOHNSTON	(Ooooooh!!)	6.4
13	JOHN BUTCHER MP	(Still trying for the chop)	6.3
14	WILLIE DONACHIE	('I just stuck my foot out, and it was there')	5.9
15	GARY SPRAKE	(He'd got to hand it to them)	5.8
16	SELINA SCOTT	(Name dropper)	5.7
17	LORD GEORGE-BROWN	(He'd got to beat Wilson in something)	5.7
18	JOHN PROFUMO	(caught and bowled Keeler)	5.5
19	SHIRLEY WILLIAMS	(Better late than never)	5.4
20	PRINCE PHILIP	(Yes, we've *all* got to pull our fingers out)	5.0

How Wrong can you Be? Just Ask the Future Merchants

Seeing Stars

In October 1977, the man who claimed he could see through anything ended up seeing stars. Illusionist Romark (real name Ronald Markham) was blindfolded and strapped into a car in busy Cranbrook Road, Ilford, London. He then set off, claiming he didn't need eyes, he could navigate with his 'psychic powers'.

But the powers which intervened were not quite as expected. For soon after Romark started driving, his yellow Renault crashed straight into the back of a police Black Maria.

At Snaresbrook Crown Court in September 1979, Romark was found guilty of reckless driving and fined £100 with £220 costs.

He told the court: 'I could see everything. My blindfold had nothing to do with it. The police van was very dangerously parked.'

Mr Stephen Hall-Jones, defending, told the jury: 'I had considered counting three, two, one then clicking my fingers – and when you woke up you would record a not-guilty verdict. But I decided against this.' Perhaps he should have tried it.

In November 1979, *The Sun* asked astrologer Roger Elliott to look ahead to the 'delights and disasters' we would face in the 1980s. Among his predictions:

POLITICS: Scotland to have total independence by 1985. The Irish problem to be solved in a close confederation between the United Kingdom, Ulster and Eire, with Eire joining the Commonwealth.

A Liberal revival, with proportional representation in elections.

Margaret Thatcher to 'move house' in October 1982.

Denis Healey to be Labour Party leader, David Owen to succeed him.

ROYALTY: Prince Charles to announce his engagement during 1980. Most likely contender: Lady Amanda Knatchbull.

The Queen to be crowned head of a United States of Europe in 1985.

SOCCER: Brian Clough to be England manager and after 1982 World Cup, also work in America.

Top British managers: Geoff Hurst, Emlyn Hughes, Terry Venables (one out of three there).

INTERNATIONAL SCENE: A United States of Europe by 1985, with one member – probably France – expelled.

Teddy Kennedy to be US President 1980–84. Richard Nixon to make a political comeback.

But clairvoyants have been getting it wrong for centuries. There was the old harridan Mother Shipton, some of whose vague predictions seem to have been borne out, if she hadn't spoiled it with:

The world then to an end shall come
In Eighteen Hundred and Eighty One.

In July 1959, a Milan doctor and forty other members of an obscure religious faith shut themselves in a cabin on Mont Blanc in the Alps, and waited for the end of the world. What they called 'voices' had told them it would happen at 1.45 p.m. that afternoon.

At 1.56 p.m. the doctor emerged. He said: 'Anybody can make a mistake.'

Another revered astrologer, Frederic Davies, predicted for 1974:

Concorde to get big orders.

Prince Charles to become engaged this year to a Taurean with the initials JM or W.

If a general election, Ted Heath to be re-elected.

President Nixon not to resign.

Mr Davies was obviously a fan of Ted Heath. On election day, 25 February 1974, he said:

'Edward Heath has chosen the perfect day for his re-election. The mood of the people as they go to the polls will be a genuine wish for a return to law and order. . . . It is the start of the way to peaceful prosperity . . . immediate problems will be solved.'

In 1978 Mr Davies said:

Miss World will be an Eskimo.

Caroline Kennedy will wed a rich Wyoming rancher in the spring.

He was still at it a year later:

President Carter will be re-elected in 1980.

Among predictions for 1979, another British stargazer, Margorie Staves, said:

Teddy Kennedy will reveal he believes in reincarnation.

and:

On her Russian husband's advice, Christina Onassis will give her massive fortune to Communism.

A couple of years later, Benjamin Creme, of Tufnell Park, north London, spent £100 000 on newspaper advertisements announcing the coming of a second Christ. The new Messiah, said Creme, would reveal himself on 21 June 1981.

Well, perhaps everyone was too busy thinking about the Royal Wedding.

In 1983, a new astrological star rose like a meteor to capture the nation's hearts and minds – the man dubbed 'the inflatable astrologer', Russell Grant.

Pudgy Russell had already had a brush with Royalty, styling himself 'Astrologer Royal' in 1980, a piece of bluff which brought the swift and cutting response from Buckingham Palace: 'Nonsense.'

Among Russell's predictions for 1980:

Edward Kennedy could win the US presidency.

A major earthquake in California.

A showdown between Britain and France.

Yorkshire Ripper caught. A town with the initial letter H will be significant in the arrest. (He was arrested in 1981 in Sheffield).

Prince Charles needs to watch his health. Something silly to happen to him, involving cars or electricity. (Luckily, no).

VAT to be removed from theatre admissions. (No again).

Marlene Dietrich to be taken ill at the end of 1980. (She was still going strong four years later.)

Olivia Newton-John to make big news in Australia. (Quite the opposite happened. Apart from spending much of the year in Malibu, the papers down-under banned her from the news columns after her manager scuffled with a photographer).

In 1974, John Gribben and Stephen Plagemann wrote a best-selling book *The Jupiter Effect* predicting horrors for 1982:

When Jupiter aligns with Mars in the early months of 1982, the Sun's activity will be at a peak ... there will be a pronounced effect on the overall circulation and on weather patterns ... there will be many earthquakes, large and small ... the San Andreas fault ... key to disaster ... most likely it will be the Los Angeles section of the fault to move. Possibly it will be the San Francisco area which has a major quake. In any case, a major earthquake will herald one of the greatest disasters of modern times.

Perhaps they meant 1992, or 2092, or 2083, or ...

Mind you, even the most celebrated in the field have been known to get it wrong. In 1939, *Old Moore's Almanac* said:

There seems good hope that peace may be preserved.

For 1966 Old Moore said:

The strong astrological influences moving through the map of England point definitely to the formation of a unified or national type of Government of all parties for the good of the country in general.

The not-always-farsighted soothsayer was at it again in 1983, predicting that an ex-astronaut would beat Ronald Reagan in the 1984 Presidential contest.

Of all the possible candidates whose charts are available the one who stands out head and shoulders this time is John Glenn.

Among other 1984 predictions:

'Important constitutional proposals' involving the Queen and Prince Charles announced in April.

Roy Jenkins 'to gain considerable authority'.

Britain to make major show of strength over the Falkland Islands in June.

Old Moore also failed to predict one of the strangest events of 1984, when crowds gathered in Leamington to witness the death and resurrection of a man claiming to be possessed with the spirit of a Muslim faith healer born in 400 AD.

Mr Malkeet Singh, of Market Street, had announced he would die on a Sunday during April at 10.45 a.m., and be reincarnated at 12.15 to the accompaniment of much dazzling light, locked doors being opened, and black and white photographs being turned to colour.

The 'miracle', as he termed it, brought people bearing gifts from as far away as Leicester and Birmingham, and a traffic jam. Police had to move in and seal off the area.

Unfortunately, the spirit had not made its appearance by 12.45 and Mr Singh asked his guests: 'Can you come back at two o'clock?'

Some called the 'miracle' 'a load of rubbish'. Others stayed through the afternoon. Mr Singh continued acting as he had been all day, that is, adopting possessed-like poses and pounding the floor with his hands.

By nightfall still nothing had happened though, and the next day Mr Singh was back at his job at the Ford foundry nearby. He told an interviewer: 'I was misled about the date.'

Clairvoyant Stanka Zarevova of Batak, Bulgaria, really slipped up in 1975 when she prescribed a cure for a spurned wife's wrinkles.

'Dip your face in the mud from the bottom of the wishing well,' Stanka told housewife Katya Tonikova, whose husband had started to chase dolly-birds.

Mrs Tonikova dipped her face in the wishing well all right . . .

and the rest of herself too. After trying to dredge up some mud for the clairvoyant's instant cure, she fell down the well.

Mrs Zarevova, 63, found herself being given three months jail for 'giving advice that might have killed her client.'

Back to another star English astrologer Maurice Woodruff. For 1972, he predicted:

Richard Nixon to just scrape in as President. (It was a landslide).

World capitals shaken by red plot. Men in half a dozen capitals named as undercover Communists. (It didn't happen.)

Concern over health of Marshal Tito. (He was fine.)

Nigel Davenport nominated for Oscar. (No he wasn't.)

Mrs Gandhi out of power. (Not in 1972.)

Tommy Cooper a new film star. (No.)

Archbishop Makarios toppled. (No again.)

Julie Andrews in top West End show. (No again.)

Russia and China close to war. (No.)

Lucille Ball to retire. (No . . . yawn . . .)

Duke of Bedford star of new TV show. (You must be joking.)

The *Sunday Times* totted up Mr Woodruff's predictions and gave him one out of sixteen . . . the banker-shot that unemployment was likely to rise during the year. (Gee whizz!)

But it's a tough business. Spare a thought for clairvoyant Kim Tracey who, in September 1983, booked for a show at Chesterfield's Pomegranate Theatre. It had to be cancelled 'due to unforseen circumstances'. No tickets were sold.

Poor Forecasting

'We have a saying in Iran,' said the Shah in 1979, 'the dogs bark but the caravan continues. People can bark and it will not bother us. Why should it?' With hindsight, of course, it should have bothered him quite a lot. History takes a terrible toll – and makes terrible fools – of those unwise enough to challenge fate.

After the war, there will be a revolution in the United States, and presumably elsewhere, coming at a time of profound economic dislocation.

Leon Trotsky, 1940

Peter Tatchell is part of the real Labour Party, and he'll be in Parliament by the end of the year.

Tony Benn, February 1983

I shall get out of acting before I am 26.

Candice Bergen, aged 21, 1967
(starred in Rich and Famous, *1981,*
aged 35, Gandhi, *1982, aged 36 . . .)*

The Duke and my daughter are good friends. A romance? Good gracious, I don't think so.

Sir William Worsley, father of the
Duchess of Kent-to-be, 1967

The truth will emerge. I will fight to prove my innocence. I intend to remain in the high office to which I was twice elected.

Spiro T. Agnew, August 1963

I am bored to tears with gossip about Ted and his so called illicit romances. They do not affect the relationship between him and me.

Mrs Joan Kennedy, October 1972

The United States will collapse by 1980.

Timothy Leary, 1965

I think when the facts come out, the President will be forgiven.

John Dean on Richard Nixon, 1973

Some sort of intuition told me that this was the girl with whom I wanted to spend the rest of my life.

James Hunt on Suzy, July 1974

I have a real chance to win this nomination.
Sen. Edward Kennedy, August 1980

15 Golden Rules for Stargazers, Seers and Soothsayers

1 Be as vague as you can. Inject as many words as you can like 'might' 'could' and 'possibly', e.g.: 'today you may find yourself doing things around the home'; 'a letter from someone distant could arrive in the post'.

2 Make as many predictions as you can – one of them in the end is bound to be right.

3 Always wear flowing gowns (or, if male, colourful bow ties) and try to talk in a high-pitched voice to give a kind of ethereal air.

4 Be careful with Royalty: never relate births specifically to one member (e.g. Princess Diana) and never try to predict whether it will be a boy or a girl. If you're vague, you're bound to get it right about some distant royal cousin . . . they're always having babies.
    Otherwise you're safe with: Prince Philip putting his foot in it; Princess Anne putting her foot in it; Prince Andrew and hints of romance; and Prince Charles falling off his horse.

5 You'll never be wrong with: A row in the Common Market, dissent in the Labour Party.

6 Another good standby: X (preferably over the age of 75 and looking frail) should look to his health. Certain astrologers have made a name for themselves by predicting the deaths of Marshal Tito, President Brezhnev, Albert Tatlock, and the world's oldest man.

7 Another good standby: there will be a coup in a country with the initial letter 'C' 'N' 'M' 'H' 'S' 'T' 'P' or 'R'. For extra accuracy and authenticity, add 'Third World' or 'by the sea'.

8   Remember, the following are the graveyard of tipsters: the second San Francisco Earthquake, the Loch Ness monster, life on Mars, Miss World, the winner of the Grand National.

9   Make sure you do separate predictions for singles and marrieds, e.g.: 'For the unattached, a lively new romance begins today; if you are married, expect a row over the washing up.'

10' Don't give anyone a cause for suicide, e.g., 'Today you will have bad news from the income tax man', 'if in business beware of sudden and unexpected bankruptcy', or 'today your partner in life will find out your guilty secret'.

11 Never prophesy a comeback, unless you are talking about Frank Sinatra, Muhammad Ali, Malcolm Allison or Tommy Docherty in which case you're pretty safe.

12 Remember there are 28 days in February, 29 in leap years. Lucky birthdays should *not* fall on February 30th and 31st.

13 Never walk under a ladder or let a black cat cross your path . . . or go out on Friday the thirteenth. If anything happens to you, you'll never live it down.

14 If you are caught out, remember: your predictions were right but your dates must have been wrong.

15 P.S.: If you do find you really have a gift for predicting the future, no kidding: don't waste a moment – start doing the football pools.

Some People's Chickens Always Come Home to Roost

More Boomerangs

'Thou *shalt* commit adultery,' said the Bible of 1631. 'Know ye not that the unrighteous shall inherit the Kingdom of God?' said the edition of 1653. Though 'Sin on more,' was perhaps its most catchy phrase.

For centuries, in every walk of life, own goals have been scored.

The Preservation Society of Charleston, South Carolina spent £25 000 renovating the historic former home of John Lining, pioneer of meteorology.

Then someone told them he had *owned the house less than 24 hours*. He went back on the deal the same day in 1730 after a dispute with the owner.

Western Union were sued in November 1983 for 'inflicting emotional pain'. Instead of sending a birthday greetings telegram saying: 'WE LOVE YOU VERY MUCH + MOM AND DAD', the wire came out as 'WE LOVE YOU VERY MUCH + MOM IS DEAD'.

Sastri Chindah, a docker of Mahe, India, was well practised in the art of getting his own way with his wife and children. He would threaten to drown himself. Everyone would then quickly give in.

Finally, of course, in July 1983, the 27 members of his family told him, 'OK, go ahead.'

They followed him to the water's edge in magnificent anticipation.

But he chickened out at the last moment. The water's-edge melodrama cost him not only his credibility – he was fined £45 for disturbing the peace.

In June 1982, a thief broke into a car belonging to SDP leader Mrs Shirley Williams while she was visiting Aston Rowant nature reserve, and stole her handbag. A police spokesman said, with total lack of aplomb: 'We are hoping that the thief will throw away the handbag when he discovers who it belongs to.'

Still with those ex-Labour ministers, the late Lord Wigg made a kindly stipulation in his will that a sum of money should be set aside and divided among his chums.

He allowed £100 each to his special friends 'to buy themselves a memento of a treasured friendship'.

Unfortunately, Lord Wigg, who died aged 82 in August 1983, made a small omission from his £250 000 will.

He forgot to name any of the friends.

Mrs Miriam Hargrave of Wakefield, Yorks., won a place in the *Guinness Book of Records* for the incredible feat of managing to fail her driving test 39 times. She passed at her 40th attempt having appeared *incognito* in another town, Harrogate, 25 miles away.

Unfortunately the real reason for her wanting a car was rather lost in the end. She had started to learn so she could take her elderly husband out for picnics. But having finally passed her test in 1970, she found she couldn't afford a car after all.

She had spent her entire £300 life savings on driving lessons.

A bizarre game of pool ended when Ken Richardson of Hemel Hempstead, Herts, celebrating his 32nd birthday in March 1977, tried to pot a perfectly normal-looking shot. Just as he was taking aim, his dentures fell out. Unfortunately, he potted them instead of the ball. To make things worse, when his 29-year-old wife Gill tried to get them out, her hand became stuck in the pocket.

Firemen had to be called to the aptly named Oddfellows Arms

to free Mrs Richardson and her husband's false teeth with washing up liquid and a power saw. She said: 'I was more concerned about his teeth than my arm. He is very sensitive about them.'

A Hampshire man was in no doubt when he came across 30 men with darkened faces huddling on the beach in the moonlight in October 1976. None said a word. Then he saw a rubber dinghy floating nearby. He crept away and raised the alarm.

Within minutes police had swooped on the strangers pouring ashore at Hayling Island.

Just one thing was wrong. They weren't illegal immigrants – they were Royal Marines on a night exercise.

The Reverend Dale Craig decided on a novel way to preach to the unconverted. He toured bars. Said 47-year-old Reverend Craig, episcopal priest of Wheeling, West Virginia, in June 1983, 'I knocked on doors and there was no one at home. I looked on in bars and they were crowded. So I took my ministry there.'

Regrettably it was Reverend Craig who became converted and he began to fall off his barstool 'pulpits'. The church cut his salary and he ended up in his new 'church' full time – behind the bar as a bartender.

Panic gripped a bank in Lozells Road, Birmingham, in October 1980, when a man with a thick 'Brummie' accent stormed in and said to the cashier: 'This is a stick up. Give me £1000.'

The alarm button was pressed but the cashier managed to keep the man talking until the police arrived and hauled him off.

It turned out the man hadn't been trying to rob the bank. He had been trying to open an account. The cashier had just not been able to make out what he was saying because of his thick nasal tones.

What exactly did he say? Said a police spokesman: 'It's hard to be sure because of his bloody awful accent.'

Crazy Own Goals

'What I don't like about politics is the disruption to one's family life,' said Cecil Parkinson, then untouched by scandal, in May 1983.

'I prefer beef,' said New Zealand Premier Robert Muldoon, turning his nose up at his nation's most famous product.

A few last memorable and crazy own goals.

> Suddenly I was subjected to a particularly nasty, totally unexpected and unprovoked attack.
> *Peter Sutcliffe, the Yorkshire Ripper,*
> *assaulted by a fellow jail inmate, April*
> *1983*

> You know, the Queen really rather likes me.
> *Koo Stark, February 1983*

> Superficiality and vulgarity, especially in women.
> *Nancy Reagan, December 1981,*
> *when asked if she had any phobias*

> Sometimes as a bit of a twit.
> *Prince Charles, asked by David Frost*
> *how he would describe himself*

Nothing really helps you face your own problems.
Anna Raeburn, agony aunt, on the
break-up of her marriage, August
1974

Murdoch is a monster.
Charles Douglas-Home, before
accepting the editorship of The Times
under the Australian tycoon

I'm glad I'm not Brezhnev. Being the Russian leader in the
Kremlin, you never know if someone's tape recording what
you say.
Richard Nixon

I have faith – trust – in human nature.
George Wallace, moments before he
was shot and paralysed, 1972

I will feel equality has arrived when we can elect to office
women who are as incompetent as some of the men who
are already there.

Maureen Reagan, the President's daughter, April 1982

My husband is taking legal advice.
Lady Denning, wife of Britain's top
judge, when his publishers threatened
to withdraw his latest book after libel
threats in June 1982

In my view he is too old for her.
Earl Spencer, overheard talking about
the engagement of his daughter Diana
to the Prince of Wales, 1981

Kilty as Charged

Farm worker John Kilty appeared in court in Manchester in February, 1969, accused of failing to pay a 8s 6d taxi fare.

'Are you guilty or not guilty', asked the clerk.

'Kilty,' said our friend. He was immediately jailed.

Mr Kilty of Levenshulme, Manchester, appealed on the grounds he was answering to his name, not pleading guilty. But the judge ruled he had made a plea, and he was ordered to serve his sentence.

A BBC film crew were delighted when they discovered a totally unmodernised pub in Wallsend – just right for the filming of a 1914 scene in the series *All Our Working Lives*. The landlord was thrilled, too. He told the brewery the cameras were coming – and they immediately arranged to modernise the interior.

Fred Wade wanted his ashes scattered over the field of his long-time idols, Queens Park Rangers. We have a problem, the club told his mourning relatives in April 1984. We now have a plastic pitch.

An animal lover didn't mind too much when he wrote off his Rover car after swerving to avoid a hedgehog in the road at Umberleigh, Devon, in June 1984. After all, he hadn't hit the poor beast. Then someone pointed out the hedgehog still hadn't moved. It had been dead for two days.

A conference on disasters due to take place in London in March 1984, had to be cancelled. The response to invitations was . . . a disaster.

Mervyn Elvey, 21, had to be rescued by three policemen when he jumped into fierce waves at Brighton to save his girlfriend's dog. The dog got ashore unaided.

After a night at the local hostelry in April 1984, Gloucester strongman Alan Humphrey tried to impress his drinking buddies by lifting up a car parked outside. There was just one problem. Inside were two policemen. They arrested him.

In a test in February 1983, 8 per cent of geography students at the University of Miami couldn't find Miami on the map.

Camden Council called a meeting in November 1983, to promote racial harmony. It ended with scuffles between black and white delegates, a Tory Councillor having a cup of coffee poured over him, his shin kicked and a microphone broken.

Martha Irving, a housewife from Southwell, Notts, put her handbag down on a charity stall during a Methodist jumble sale in August 1983. It contained £155 in cash.

When she returned a few seconds later, the handbag had been sold for 20 pence.

After injuring her ankle in a road accident in 1983, prostitute 'Emanuela' of Vienna successfully sued the car driver for loss of earnings. She claimed her business had suffered because she was only able to limp, not walk round the streets.

Her euphoria was shortlived. Shortly afterwards, the taxman sent a demand of £7000 for her estimated earnings as declared in court.

Mrs Solly Solomons, a South African, drove out to look for her husband when he was late home from a night out with the boys in November 1983.

As she reversed she drove over the slumbering form of Mr Solomons, who had not quite made it to the front door. He was taken to hospital seriously injured.

Norwegian health club boss Olaf Knudson had a novel diet that was a hit with his male members in the summer of 1983. For it included beer and ice cream.

Unfortunately for Olaf, as his clients got heavier and heavier, their patience wore thin.

They arrived late one night and burned down his clinic.

In August 1983 New York police had to mount a search for a lifesize bust of master escapologist Harry Houdini.

Formerly adorning his grave, the sculpture had suddenly and inexplicably . . . disappeared.

Another vanishing act . . . in July 1983. Lester Sharpe and Iris, magician and assistant, stunned regulars and staff at the Morecambe Superdrome by managing to disappear for two whole hours.

Staff found them locked in their dressing room.

And finally, company director Mr Clive Buxton, of Colwick, Nottingham, who experienced that sad happening that we all dread. He became trapped in the lavatory at his firm's offices.

The high point during his four-hour ordeal in August 1983, came when Mr Buxton managed to attract the attention of a driver of a passing car by waving frantically through the narrow window.

The motorist gave a cheery wave back and drove off.